The Philosophical Writings of

CHAUNCEY WRIGHT

The American Heritage Series

OSKAR PIEST, *General Editor*

[NUMBER TWENTY-THREE]

The Philosophical Writings of

CHAUNCEY WRIGHT

The Philosophical Writings of
CHAUNCEY WRIGHT

Representative Selections

Edited, with an Introduction, by
EDWARD H. MADDEN
Assistant Professor of Philosophy, University of Connecticut

THE LIBERAL ARTS PRESS
NEW YORK

Library of Congress Catalog Card Number 58-9962

Published at 153 West 72nd Street, New York 23, N. Y.

Printed in the United States of America

TABLE OF CONTENTS

THE PHILOSOPHICAL WRITINGS OF CHAUNCEY WRIGHT

EDITOR'S INTRODUCTION

I

Chauncey Wright was the senior member of the discussion group—C. S. Peirce later called it "The Metaphysical Club"—which met in Cambridge, Massachusetts, in the early 1870's. The membership of the club included, besides Wright, C. S. Peirce, William James, Oliver Wendell Homes, Jr., Nicholas St. John Green, and, occasionally, John Fiske and F. E. Abbot. Wright was the whetstone on which the younger men sharpened their philosophical wit; and Peirce, James, and Holmes—and many others outside the discussion group—acknowledged him to be their intellectual "boxing master" and respected mentor.

Wright's contributions to philosophy of science, ethics, and metaphysics—in the form of articles, reviews, and letters—are considerable; and within the last twenty years the historical importance and intrinsic merit of his writings have become increasingly recognized. We have, in fact, in the judgment of intrinsic merit simply recovered the original estimate of his contemporaries. Like them, one feels, reading Wright's work, not only the effects of a keenly analytical mind but also the effects of a sensitivity and honesty of inquiry that equals John Stuart Mill's. In addition, to us, his works appear surprisingly modern in tone and interest value.

Wright's work, until now, has not been readily available. His *Philosophical Discussions* and *Letters* are long out of print, and only a small number of each was printed in the first place. Moreover, his essays, reprinted in *Philosophical Discussions,* are generally long book reviews, and his own important and original ideas are often obscured by a host of detailed references to items of purely local interest—a difficulty which I have tried to remedy in the present edition of his work.

While Wright's ideas are important and original, they stand

in stark contrast to his life. In his autobiographical sketch for the *Harvard Class Book of 1858* he wrote,[1] "From the earliest period of my conscious life I have shrunk from everything of a startling or dramatic character. I was indisposed to active exercise, to any kind of excitement or change." That this attitude persisted is evident from the uneventful character of his later life. From 1852 to 1870, he was a computer for the *Nautical Almanac;* he lectured twice at Harvard College—in philosophy and psychology in 1870 and in mathematical physics in 1874—and occasionally tutored private pupils; in 1860 he was elected a fellow of the Academy of Arts and Sciences, of which he was, for a time, secretary; he visited Darwin in England in 1872; and between 1864 and 1875 he contributed numerous articles to the *North American Review* and the *Nation.* Charles Eliot Norton published Wright's essays posthumously in 1877 under the title *Philosophical Discussions.* James Bradley Thayer published his *Letters* posthumously in 1878.

II

While Wright did not collate his philosophical ideas in any systematic way, nevertheless he supplied a coherent and related set of answers to fundamental problems in all the major areas of philosophical thought. The most advantageous spot to enter into his network of ideas, I believe, is his "philosophy of science," since he developed several of his controlling concepts in this area.

The term "philosophy of science" is ambiguous, to be sure—in fact, any reflection whatever *about* science seems, in one place or another, to qualify as a "philosophy of science"—but Wright meant by it something perfectly precise, namely, an analysis of the logical structure of scientific concepts and principles. While Wright was convinced that the logical analysis of scientific principles is intrinsically important, he was particu-

[1] Chauncey Wright was born in Northampton, Massachusetts, on September 20, 1830; he died in Cambridge, Massachusetts, on September 12, 1875.

larly interested to point up, through such analysis, the pointlessness of appropriating scientific principles for partisan purposes in religion, morality, and metaphysics. As far as Wright was concerned, Herbert Spencer was the great offender on this score. Spencer's appropriation of scientific principles, he claimed, is really alien to the fundamental nature of these principles. According to Wright, nothing justifies the development of abstract principles in science but their utility in enlarging our concrete knowledge of nature. "The ideas on which mathematical mechanics and the calculus are founded, the morphological ideas of natural history, and the theories of chemistry are such working ideas—finders, not merely summaries of truth." [2] But, Wright claims, this is not the value which we find in Spencer's speculations. For example, Spencer defines psychology as the study of ideas and posits as the test of the reality of an idea "the inconceivableness of its negation." Wright points out that Spencer makes little explicit use of his postulate: "It is one of those unproductive principles which Positivism condemns; and he develops others equally useless, except in the mental discipline there may be in following their evolution." [3] Moreover, he says, Spencer adds a new sense, or rather a vagueness, to all the ideas which he adopts from science so as to make them descriptive of as much as possible. One example of this procedure is his translation of the physicist's "conservation of force" into the "persistence of force." But in losing their precision and definiteness, Wright continues, scientific principles lose their predictive value, their capacity to discover new facts (as the law of gravity led to the discovery of Uranus), in which their real value lies.

> Terms which the real physicist knows how to use as the terms of mathematical formulas . . . , terms which have been of inestimable service both in formulating and finding out the secrets of nature, are appropriated by Mr. Spencer to the further elaboration of his vague definitions, and to the abstract description of as much in real nature as they may

[2] *Philosophical Discussions,* p. 56.
[3] *Ibid.,* p. 66.

happen to apply to. . . . Out of mathematical formulas these terms lose their definiteness and their utility.[4]

Some pragmatic philosophers who came after Wright generalized his "working idea" or "working hypothesis" interpretation of scientific principles into a conception or "theory" of the nature of mind.[5] According to this view, all ideas are working hypotheses; all thinking is experimental, and scientific experimentation, in so far as it has ideal controls, is simply a limiting case of thinking. According to this "instrumental" version of pragmatism, mind, on all biological levels, functionally considered, is a tool for resolving problematic situations and ordering further experience. This conception of the mind is the pragmatist's attempt at solving "Darwin's problem" of bridging the supposed evolutionary gap between animal and human intelligence. One cannot say, however, as some commentators suggest,[6] that Wright held this pragmatic viewpoint, since his denial of the "summary" view of ideas and his assertion that they are "working hypotheses" always remain within a scientific framework and never extend to thought in general; and indeed it appears certain that Wright, unlike all the pragmatists, would have denied that a simple empirical assertion like "This diamond is hard" is an hypothesis and would, in some sense, interpret it as a summary statement.[7]

In his later years, Wright became more and more interested in analyzing the nature and explanatory function of the

[4] *Ibid.*, p. 76.

[5] I have in mind particularly John Dewey whose extensive work is best exemplified, perhaps, in his *Quest for Certainty* (New York, 1929). However, cf. also Charles S. Peirce, *Collected Papers,* Vol. V., 403.

[6] E.g., Sidney Ratner, "Evolution and the Rise of the Scientific Spirit in America," *Philosophy of Science,* III (1936), pp. 104-22. The characterizations of Wright's work go full circle: from "worker on the path opened by Hume" through "precursor of pragmatism" to "founder of pragmatism" and back again to "positivistic empiricist." I have tried to adjust these conflicting claims in my "Pragmatism, Positivism, and Chauncey Wright," *Philosophy and Phenomenological Research,* XIV (1953), pp. 62-71.

[7] Cf. Edward H. Madden, "Pragmatism, Positivism, and Chauncey Wright," *Philosophy and Phenomenological Research,* XIV (1953), pp. 62-71.

"palaetiological" sciences, that is, sciences like geology, geophysics, and certain areas of biology, which deal with concrete series of events rather than with experimentally isolated and controlled systems. His analysis in this area yielded some of the most interesting concepts of his philosophy of science, namely, "causal complexity," "irregularity," "accident," and "cosmic weather"—concepts which also played an important role in his cosmological theory.

In "The Genesis of Species," a defense of Darwin's explanation of the origin of biological species against the Jesuit naturalist St. George Mivart, Wright said that natural selection, while it imitates mechanics in isolating and separating causes under controlled conditions—for example, in experimentation with domesticated plants and animals—nevertheless should not be compared as an explanation of the origin of species with mechanics but rather with geology, meteorology, and political science, all of which exhibit causal complexity and irregularity. The only genuine explanation in these sciences, Wright urged, is the deduction as far as possible of the concrete series from combinations of elementary laws discovered in control situations. "As far as possible" is an important consideration. In a concrete series of events causal chains are intermingled most intimately; and this complexity, unfathomed in precise detail, generally gives the appearance, but the appearance only, of irregularity in concrete events.

The occurrence of an event in a concrete series of events is explained, Wright believed, when it is deductively derived from fixed principles or laws together with a statement about a previous event in the series. An event in a concrete series is called an "accident" only when its occurrence, in turn, cannot be derived or predicted—which is frequently the case, again, as a result of the causal complexity in any concrete series. This unpredictability is Darwin's meaning of "accident," which notion, unfortunately, Wright said, is oftentimes erroneously interpreted as uncaused. "In referring any effect to 'accident,' [Darwin] only means that its causes are like particular phases of the weather, or like innumerable phenomena in the concrete course of nature generally, which are quite beyond the power of finite minds to anticipate or account for in general, though none the less really determinate or due to regular causes."[8] "Accident," then, is not a characteristic of events but of our knowledge of them; it does not mean that events are uncaused but that we do not know the cause.

Wright believed, in short, what Peirce later denied, that the universality of causality is a postulate of scientific inquiry; he was, to use Peirce's terminology, a "necessitarian." Peirce wrote, "When I ask the necessitarian how he would explain the . . . irregularity of the universe, he replies to me out of the treasury of his wisdom that irregularity is something which from the nature of things we must not seek to explain."[9] On the contrary, for Wright, since irregularity is a function of causal complexity, it is a remnant that always challenges further explanation; and even in the cases where an explanation is impossible one can sometimes give what appears to be a reasonable explanatory sketch.

Cosmological speculation about the production of solar systems, or systems of worlds, Wright thought, also belongs to the palaetiological category of science. The cosmogonist uses the laws of physics, particularly the principles of gravity and thermodynamics, discovered in controlled situations, to explain the physical history of the system of worlds where there has been an uncontrolled, complex interpenetration of the principles at work. The result of this causal complexity, again, is apparent irregularity. "The constitution of the solar system is not archetypal, as the ancients supposed, but the same corrupt mixture of law and apparent accident that the phenomena of the earth's surface exhibit. . . ."[10] This irregularity rather than regularity, Wright urged against Laplace, is the proper evidence that the solar system is a product of physical or natural causes and not the result of a creative fiat.

Wright referred to the production of systems of worlds as

[8] *Philosophical Discussions,* p. 131.
[9] *Collected Papers,* Vol. 6, paragraph 60.
[10] *Philosophical Discussions,* p. 9.

"cosmic weather" and he hit upon this colorful metaphor since ordinary weather phenomena exhibit the same logical features of causal complexity and apparent irregularity, and the effort to predict them runs into the same difficulties as the cosmogonist's effort to explain the production of systems of worlds. But the metaphor meant more than this for Wright; he believed that the production of systems of worlds, like ordinary weather, shows on the whole no development or any discernible tendency whatever but is a doing and undoing without end—a kind of weather, cosmic weather. Wright based his ateleological view on what he called the principle of countermovements, "a principle in accordance with which there is no action in nature to which there is not some counter-action," which he contended is a likely generalization from the laws and facts of science.

Beginning with this concept of countermovements, he worked out a technical and elaborate hypothesis (not included in the present selections) about the nature of cosmic weather.[11] Quite briefly, impressed with the conservation of energy principle, he accounted for the origin of the sun's heat and the positions and movements of planets by the first law of thermodynamics and the conservation of angular momentum. The spiral fall of meteors into the sun, he thought, is the cause of its heat. The sun does not rapidly increase in size, he suggested, because the heat of the sun is reconverted into mechanical energy. Part of the heat is consumed in vaporizing the meteors and parts of the mass of the sun, while the rest is expended in further heating, expanding, and thus lifting the gaseous material to the heights from whence it spiraled into the sun. There it cools and condenses and the cycle begins again.

Wright apparently thought that mechanical energy and heat energy are not only convertible but reversible. However, he was not unaware of the second law of thermodynamics; at least not when he wrote "The Philosophy of Herbert Spencer" a year later. In a section of this article devoted to the nebular hypothesis Wright says that the most obvious objection to his hypothesis is Thomson's theory that there is a universal tend-

[11] *Ibid.*, pp. 17-34.

ency in nature to the dissipation of mechanical energy, "a theory well founded, nay, demonstrated, if we only follow this energy as far as the present limits of science extend. But to a true Aristotelian this theory, so far from suggesting a dramatic *denouément,* such as the ultimate death of nature, only propounds new problems. What becomes of the sun's dynamic energy, and whence do the bodies come which support this wasting power?" [12]

III

The best introduction to Wright's religious, moral, and metaphysical philosophy is his empirical view of knowledge: we should try continually, he said, to test and correct our beliefs by the particulars of concrete experience of a kind common to all. (Note Wright's emphasis on the empirical *verification* of beliefs, not on their empirical *origin*—an important shift from traditional English empiricism toward modern empiricism.)

Religious beliefs, Wright averred, are based on private religious insights, or else on mere authority—whether the authority be external or simply one's own driving desire for the beliefs to be true—and so they cannot, of course, be tested or corrected in this fashion. Consequently he denied that religious beliefs can properly be called *knowledge,* although he admitted they may be rightfully accepted as tenets of *faith* by anyone so inclined. Wright, in short, was an agnostic or religious skeptic who was, as J. B. Thayer wrote, interested neither to prove nor disprove (in the advocate's sense) but to judge; and when there is insufficient material for judging, to hold his mind in suspense—a suspense, however, which contains no element of pain. Of Wright's agnosticism, William James (who spent the rest of his life trying to escape it) wrote, "Never in a human head was contemplation more separated from desire." Astonishing as it may seem, Wright simply had few desires one way or another about God.

Wright's utilitarian moral philosophy and criticism of intuition and conscience theories also resulted from his empirical

[12] *Ibid.,* p. 87.

view of knowledge. The utilitarian judges an act right if it leads to certain good consequences, namely, general welfare, or the greatest happiness for the greatest number; and, conversely, judges an act wrong if it leads to consequences of a generally unfortunate sort. Since Wright felt that moral judgments based on an examination of consequences, unlike the deliverances of "intuition" or "conscience," lend themselves to test and correction by common or "public" experience, he accepted the utilitarian tradition in moral philosophy. He strongly believed that the principle of utility is crucially important in practice as the standard for correcting a whole world of abuses which subsist by the very same sanctions the intuitive morality adopts as the basis of right and wrong. Self-sanctioned prejudices, time-sanctioned iniquities, and religious absurdities are abuses "which can claim the same grounds of justification as those on which the intuitive morality would base the ten commandments; namely, that most people, or at least somebody, *feels* them to be right." [13]

Wright clearly followed J. S. Mill in distinguishing qualitative differences among pleasures. In his *Utilitarianism* Mill had introduced the notion that spiritual pleasures are intrinsically better than sensuous ones, and Wright, too, insisted that certain pleasures have "a high rank, an intrinsic dignity or preferability in kind." These ranks or differences, however, are not moral ones. They are simply ends in themselves or sources of happiness, whereas moral value, what one ought to do or ought to desire, is a derived problem, "determined by preferability or weight with the will on the whole and as compared with the *sum* of the pleasures or ends that are sacrificed for it, both in ourselves and others." [14] In this discussion Wright is making, more clearly and carefully than J. S. Mill, the utilitarian distinction between "intrinsic good" and "ought." In addition, he urged that utility, conceived as a *test* or standard of conduct, must be supplemented by a philosophy of "habit" that recognizes the practical necessity and importance of non-calcula-

[13] *Letters,* p. 197.
[14] *Ibid.,* p. 195.

tional behavior. He defended the principle of utility against a wide variety of criticisms and applied it, in detail, to such pressing moral concerns of his day as the "privileges" of wealth (on which he took a more radical stand for curtailment than Mill), the rights of women, political liberty, and the nature and need of self-sacrifice.

Metaphysical questions—like "Does anything exist by itself independently of its effect on us?"—which cannot in principle be tested or corrected are *closed questions,* Wright said, that is, questions of which we are ignorant beyond the possibility of enlightenment. To the metaphysicians' criticism of the empiricists for not answering them, Wright replied that they are idle and gratuitous since they could not in principle ever be answered. Now this exclusion of metaphysical questions as pointless or gratuitous does not mean that Wright any more than Hume or J. S. Mill ignored certain problems which other philosophers, called "metaphysicians," dealt with. For example, they, just like other philosophers, dealt with the problem of whether or not one can legitimately assert the existence of an object when it is unperceived. They simply denied that it is meaningful to assert the existence of an object as *unconditionally* independent of perception. What one must mean by saying an object exists when unperceived, Mill said and Wright agreed, is that *if* one were to go and look, one *would* receive certain perceptions. This permanent possibility of perception, not simply actual perception, forms the meaning of "the existence of an unperceived object."

The metaphysical concepts which most interested Wright were "self-consciousness," "a priori knowledge," and "space" and "time," which is indeed unusual since these concepts are the very ones most nineteenth century empiricists and positivists liked to avoid wherever possible. In his analysis of the structure of self-consciousness, Wright, after sketching a naturalistic account of the origin of self-consciousness, tried to show that the notion of substance in "mental substance" (and "physical substance" too) is a meaningless term and arises from the misleading nature of the syntax of natural languages. He believed, rather, that there are only neutral "phenomena" and that the distinction of subject and object is a classification of phenomena through observation and analysis and not, as the metaphysician claims, an intuitive and irreducible distinction. Wright's position here is essentially a *neutral monism* and is a precursor of William James' notion of "pure experience" which he presents in *Essays in Radical Empiricism,* although, as one might expect, there are many differences too.[15]

In his analysis of a priori knowledge, Wright did not claim, as the nineteenth century empiricists usually did, that there is no a priori knowledge or that a priori knowledge is always analytic. He insisted, on the contrary, that *all* knowledge, even perception of qualities as well as relations and so-called higher knowledge, has an a priori element, and this element can be explained experientially. This analysis is particularly interesting at the present time since we are currently offered all sorts of "factual" and "pragmatic" concepts of a priori knowledge.

Wright, it should be noted finally, devoted a good part of his metaphysical writing to negative criticism of the work of the Scottish realists. For example, Wright thought that James McCosh erred in trying to solve philosophical problems by recourse to common-sense beliefs. McCosh's appeal from the skeptic's questions (e.g., Is inductive inference justifiable? or Are any truths necessary?) to common sense is irrelevant because the doubts of the skeptic do not concern questions of fact but their proper interpretation. The skeptic, for example, does not deny that many of his beliefs are necessary; what he does deny is the ascription of this necessity to intuitive simplicity. The skeptic's doubts and questions about metaphysical truths are doubts and questions not about the reality of these knowledges but about the *kind* of reality they have.

> It is common, indeed, in physical investigations to speak of an appeal to experiment or to observation; still, by this is meant, not an appeal from anybody's decision or opinion, but from everybody's ignorance of the facts of the case. The facts

[15] Cf. Edward H. Madden, "Wright, James, and Radical Empiricism," *The Journal of Philosophy,* LI (1954), pp. 868-874.

> in philosophy are so notorious that this sort of appeal is not required. What is sought by the so-called "sceptic" is the *nature* of the fact, its explanation; . . . In this the idealist does not deny that there is an existence properly enough called the external world, but he wishes to ascertain the nature of this reality by studying what the notion of externality really implies; what are the circumstances attending its rise in our thoughts, and its probable growth in our experience.[16]

Wright disagreed, in short, with the members of the whole Scottish school who thought the business of philosophy is to scrutinize truths as to their credibility: "As if truths were on trial for their lives! As if the 'sceptic' desired worse of them than their better acquaintance!"

Wright's view of ordinary knowledge might well be summed up in this way: ordinary knowledge must be explained or interpreted by *any* philosophical system if that system is to be acceptable but it does not itself constitute a resolution or dissolution of any philosophical problem. This view is not only a widely held one at the present time but is, finally, I believe, the only fruitful one to hold, since the only alternatives are to accept philosophical assertions like "Time is unreal" or "Motion is impossible" or "There are no physical objects" as literally true, and so violate common sense, which indeed seems pointless, or else to assert, in the other extreme, that philosophical assertions are simply unwarranted perversions of common sense or ordinary discourse, which is indeed difficult to justify.

Wright, on the other hand, defended the Scottish realists and their view of ordinary knowledge against what he considered occasional misinterpretation by Mill and F. E. Abbot. In fact, both in his polemical and original work, Wright unfailingly tried to do justice to the subtleties of contending views. One might say of him, as he said of Mill, "he weighed his arguments as dispassionately as if his aim had been pure science . . . and sincerely welcomed intelligent and earnest opposition with a

16 *Philosophical Discussions,* p. 339.

deference due to truth itself."[17] Charles Eliot Norton, Wright's closest friend in later years, summed up the matter in a striking way: "To argue with him was a moral no less than an intellectual discipline."[18]

EDWARD H. MADDEN

[17] *Ibid.*, pp. 415, 417.
[18] *Ibid.*, p. xii.

NOTE ON THE TEXT

This text follows the original texts—for Wright's essays, *The North American Review;* for his letters, the handwritten originals in the Houghton Library, Harvard University. I gratefully acknowledge permission of the Librarian of Houghton Library to reproduce Wright's original letters.

Wright's letters to Francis E. Abbot are an exception. Since the originals of these letters are unavailable, this text follows James B. Thayer's (*Letters of Chauncey Wright,* Cambridge, 1878).

The original texts have been reproduced with occasional modification in punctuation and capitalization. Several selections consist of parts taken from different sources—which fact, whenever it occurs, is evident from a multiple footnote reference. The titles, notes, and explanations which the editor has supplied are enclosed by brackets.

E.H.M.

SELECTED BIBLIOGRAPHY

Works of Chauncey Wright

Letters. Edited by James Bradley Thayer. Cambridge, 1878.

"Letters to Charles Eliot Norton, Grace Norton, and Jane Norton." Harvard College Library (Houghton), bMs Am 1088, 1088.1.

Philosophical Discussions. Edited by Charles Eliot Norton. New York, 1877.

Collateral Reading

Anderson, Paul R. and Max H. Fisch. *Philosophy in America.* New York and London, 1939.

Blau, Joseph L. "Chauncey Wright: Radical Empiricist," *New England Quarterly,* XIX (1946), 495-517.

——. *Men and Movements in American Philosophy.* New York, 1952.

Bowne, Borden Parker. "Chauncey Wright as a Philosopher," *New Englander,* XXXVII (1878), 585-603.

Cohen, Morris. "Charles S. Peirce and a Tentative Bibliography of His Published Writings," *Journal of Philosophy,* XIII (1916), 726-737.

——. Introduction to *Chance, Love, and Logic.* New York, 1923.

——. "Later Philosophy," *The Cambridge History of American Literature* (New York, 1921), II, 226-265.

Fisch, Max. "Evolution in American Philosophy," *Philosophical Review,* LVI (1947), 357-373.

——. Introduction to *Classic American Philosophers.* New York, 1951.

Fiske, John. *Darwinism, and Other Essays.* New York, 1888.

James, William. "Brute and Human Intellect," *Journal of Speculative Philosophy,* XII (1878), 236-276.

——. *Collected Essays and Reviews.* New York, 1920.

James (cont'd). *Essays in Radical Empiricism.* New York, 1922.

———. *Principles of Psychology.* 2 vols. New York, 1890.

Kennedy, Gail. "The Pragmatic Naturalism of Chauncey Wright," in *Studies in the History of Ideas,* III, edited by the Department of Philosophy, Columbia University. New York, 1935.

Madden, Edward H. "The Cambridge Septem," *Harvard Alumni Bulletin,* LVII (1955), 310-315.

———. "Chauncey Wright: Forgotten American Philosopher," *American Quarterly,* IV (1952), 25-34.

———. "Chauncey Wright's Life and Work: Some New Material," *Journal of the History of Ideas,* XV (1954), 445-455.

———. "Pragmatism, Positivism, and Chauncey Wright," *Philosophy and Phenomenological Research,* XIV (1953), 62-71.

———. "Wright, James, and Radical Empiricism," *Journal of Philosophy,* LI (1954), 868-874.

———. "Chance and Counterfacts in Wright and Peirce," *The Review of Metaphysics,* IX (1956), 420-432.

——— and Marian C. Madden. "Chauncey Wright and the Logic of Psychology," *Philosophy of Science,* XIX (1952), 325-332.

Peirce, Charles Sanders. *Collected Papers.* Edited by Charles Hartshorne and Paul Weiss. Cambridge, 1931-35.

Perry, Ralph Barton. *Annotated Bibliography of the Writings of William James.* New York, 1920.

———. *Thought and Character of William James.* 2 vols. Boston, 1935.

Ratner, Sidney. "Evolution and the Rise of the Scientific Spirit in America," *Philosophy of Science,* III (1939), 104.

Schneider, Herbert W. *A History of American Philosophy.* New York, 1946.

Wiener, Philip P. "Chauncey Wright's Defense of Darwin and the Neutrality of Science," *Journal of the History of Ideas,* VI (1945), 19-45.

———. *Evolution and the Founders of Pragmatism.* Cambridge, 1949.

The Philosophical Writings of

CHAUNCEY WRIGHT

I

PHILOSOPHY OF SCIENCE

[THE ORIGINS OF MODERN SCIENCE][1]

Why the inductive and mathematical sciences, after their first rapid development at the culmination of Greek civilization, advanced so slowly for two thousand years—and why in the following two hundred years a knowledge of natural and mathematical science has accumulated which so vastly exceeds all that was previously known that these sciences may be justly regarded as the products of our own times—are questions which have interested the modern philosopher not less than the objects with which these sciences are more immediately conversant. Was it in the employment of a new method of research, or in the exercise of greater virtue in the use of old methods, that this singular modern phenomenon had its origin? Was the long period one of arrested development, and is the modern era one of a normal growth? Or should we ascribe the characteristics of both periods to inexplicable historical accidents—to the influence of conjunctions in circumstances of which no explanation is possible save in the omnipotence and wisdom of a guiding Providence?

The explanation which has become commonplace, that the ancients employed deduction chiefly in their scientific inquiries while the moderns employ induction, proves to be too narrow, and fails upon close examination to point with sufficient distinctness the contrast that is evident between ancient and modern scientific doctrines and inquiries. For all knowledge is founded on observation, and proceeds from this by analysis and synthesis, by synthesis and analysis, by induction and deduction,

[1] [*North American Review*, C (1865), 423-432.]

and if possible by verification, or by new appeals to observation under the guidance of deduction—by steps which are indeed correlative parts of one method; and the ancient sciences afford examples of every one of these methods, or parts of the one complete method, which have been generalized from the examples of science.

A failure to employ or to employ adequately any one of these partial methods, an imperfection in the arts and resources of observation and experiment, carelessness in observation, neglect of relevant facts, vagueness and carelessness in reasoning, and the failure to draw the consequences of theory and test them by appeal to experiment and observation—these are the faults which cause all failures to ascertain truth, whether among the ancients or the moderns; but they do not explain why the modern is possessed of a greater virtue, and by what means he attained to his superiority. Much less do they explain the sudden growth of science in recent times.

The attempt to discover the explanation of this phenomenon in the antithesis of "facts" and "theories" or "facts" and "ideas" —in the neglect among the ancients of the former, and their too exclusive attention to the latter—proves also to be too narrow, as well as open to the charge of vagueness. For, in the first place, the antithesis is not complete. Facts and theories are not co-ordinate species. Theories, if true, are facts—a particular class of facts indeed, generally complex ones, but still facts. Facts, on the other hand, even in the narrowest signification of the word, if they be at all complex and if a logical connection subsists between their constituents, have all the positive attributes of theories.

Nevertheless, this distinction, however inadequate it may be to explain the source of true method in science, is well founded, and connotes an important character in true method. A fact is a proposition of which the verification by an appeal to the primary sources of our knowledge or to experience is direct and simple. A theory, on the other hand, if true, has all the characteristics of a fact except that its verification is possible only by indirect, remote, and difficult means. To convert theories into facts is to add *simple verification*, and the theory thus acquires the full characteristics of a fact. When Pascal caused the Torricellian tube [2] to be carried up the Puy de Dôme, and thus showed that the mercurial column was sustained by the weight of the atmosphere, he brought the theory of atmospheric pressure nearly down to the level of a fact of observation. But even in this most remarkable instance of scientific discovery theory was not wholly reduced to fact, since the verification, though easy, was not entirely simple, and was incomplete until further observations showed that the quantity of the fall in the Torricellian tube agreed with deductions from the combined theories of atmospherical pressure and elasticity. In the same way the theory of universal gravitation fails to become a fact in the proper sense of this word, however complete its verification, because this verification is not simple and direct, or through the spontaneous activity of our perceptive powers.

Modern science deals, then, no less with theories than with facts, but always as much as possible with the verification of theories—if not to make them facts by *simple* verification through experiment and observation, at least to prove their truth by indirect verification.

The distinction of fact and theory thus yields an important principle, of which M. Comte [3] and his followers have made

[2] [Blaise Pascal (1623-1662), French philosopher, mathematician, and scientist. "The idea of the pressure of the air and the invention of the instrument for measuring it were both new when he made his famous experiment, showing that the height of the mercury column in a barometer decreases when it is carried upwards through the atmosphere. This experiment was made by himself in a tower at Paris, and was carried out on a grand scale under his instructions by his brother-in-law Florin Périer on the Puy de Dôme in Auvergne. Its success greatly helped . . . to bring home to the minds of ordinary men the truth of the new ideas propounded by Galileo and Torricelli." *Encyclopaedia Britannica*, 1957. Vol. 17, p. 351.]

[3] [Auguste Comte (1798-1857), French philosopher and mathematician. See his major work, *Course of Positive Philosophy*, an influential work in nineteenth century philosophy, for the ideas to which Wright refers.]

much account. It is in the employment of verification, they say, and in the possibility of it, that the superiority of modern inductive research consists; and it is because the ancients did not, or could not, verify their theories that they made such insignificant progress in science. It is indisputable that verification is essential to the completeness of scientific method; but there is still room for debate as to what constitutes verification in the various departments of philosophical inquiry. So long as the philosophy of method fails to give a complete inventory of our primary sources of knowledge and cannot decide authoritatively what are the origins of first truths or the truths of observation, so long will it remain uncertain what is a legitimate appeal to observation or what is a real verification. The Platonists or the rationalists may equally with the empiricists claim verification for their theories; for do they not appeal to the reason for confirmation of deductions from their theories, which they regard as founded on observation of what the reason reveals to them?

The positivists' principle of verification comes, then, only to this—that, inasmuch as mankind are nearly unanimous about the testimony and trustworthiness of their senses, but are divided about the validity of all other kinds of authority, which they in a word call the reason or internal sense, therefore verification by the senses produces absolute conviction while verification by the reason settles nothing, but is liable to the same uncertainty which attends the primary appeals to this authority for the data of speculative knowledge.

But not only does the so-called metaphysical philosophy employ a species of verification by appealing to the testimony of reason, consciousness, or internal sense, but the ancient physical sciences afford examples of the confirmation of theory by observation proper. The Ptolemaic system of astronomy was an instance of the employment of every one of the partial steps of true method; and the theory of epicycles not only sought to represent the facts of observation but also by the prediction of astronomical phenomena to verify the truth of its representation. Modern astronomy does not proceed otherwise, except that its theories represent a much greater number of facts of observation and are confirmed by much more efficient experimental tests.

The difference, then, between ancient and modern science is not truly characterized by any of the several explanations which have been proposed. The explanation which, in our opinion, comes nearer to the true solution, and yet fails to designate the real point of difference, is that which the positivists find in the distinction between "objective method" and "subjective method." The objective method is verification by sensuous tests, tests of sensible experience—a deduction from theory to consequences, of which we may have sensible experiences if they be true. The subjective method, on the other hand, appeals to the tests of internal evidence, tests of reason, and the data of self-consciousness—authorities on which, as the history of philosophy shows, there is little unanimity among philosophers. But whatever be the origin of the theories of science, whether from a systematic examination of empirical facts by conscious induction or from the natural biases of the mind, the so-called intuitions of reason, what seems probable without a distinct survey of our experiences—whatever the origin, real or ideal, the *value* of these theories can only be tested, say the positivists, by an appeal to sensible experience, by deductions from them of consequences which we can confirm by the undoubted testimony of the senses. Thus, while ideal or transcendental elements are admitted into scientific researches, though in themselves insusceptible of simple verification, they must still show credentials from the senses, either by affording from themselves consequences capable of sensuous verification or by yielding such consequences in conjunction with ideas which by themselves are verifiable.

It is undoubtedly true that one of the leading traits of modern scientific research is this reduction of ideas to the tests of experience. The systematic development of ideas through induction from the first and simplest facts of observation is by no means so obvious a characteristic. Inductions are still performed for the most part unconsciously and unsystematically. Ideas are developed by the sagacity of the expert rather than by the systematic procedures of the philosopher. But when and however ideas are developed science cares nothing, for it is only by subsequent tests of sensible experience that ideas are admitted into the pandects of science.

It is of no consequence to scientific astronomy whence the theory of gravitation arose, whether as an induction from the theories of attractions and the law of radiations or from the rational simplicity of this law itself as the most natural supposition which could be made. Science asks no questions about the ontological pedigree or a priori character of a theory, but is content to judge it by its performance; and it is thus that a knowledge of nature, having all the certainty which the senses are competent to inspire, has been attained—a knowledge which maintains a strict neutrality toward all philosophical systems and concerns itself not at all with the genesis or a priori grounds of ideas.

This mode of philosophizing is not, however, exclusively found in modern scientific research. Ptolemy[4] claimed for his epicycles only that "they saved the appearances"; and he might have said, with as much propriety as Newton,[5] *Hypotheses non fingo,* for it was the aim of his research to represent abstractly, and by the most general formulas, the characteristics of the movements of the planets—an aim which modern astronomy, with a much simpler hypothesis and with immensely increased facilities, still pursues.

We find, therefore, that while moderns follow a true method of investigation with greater facilities and greater fidelity than the ancients, and with a clearer apprehension of its elements

4 [Ptolemy of Alexandria (second century A.D.), astronomer, mathematician, and geographer. For a straightforward explanation of "epicycle," "eccentric," and "equant," fundamental concepts in his geocentric astronomical theory, see *Encyclopaedia Britannica,* 1957, Vol. 2, p. 582. His major astronomical work is the *Syntaxis* or *Almagest.*]

5 [Sir Isaac Newton (1642-1727), English physicist and mathematician. For an analysis of Newton's philosophy of science, including his famous dictum *Hypotheses non fingo,* see Chapter 6 of *Theories of Scientific Method from the Renaissance to the Nineteenth Century,* R. W. Blake, C. J. Ducasse, and E. H. Madden, University of Washington Press, 1958.]

and conditions, yet that no new discoveries in method have been made, and no general sources of truth have been pointed out, which were not patent and known to the ancients; and we have so far failed to discover any solution to the problem with which we began. We have seen that it was not by the employment of a new method of research, but in the exercise of greater virtue in the use of old methods, that modern scientific researches have succeeded. But whence this greater virtue? What vivifying, energizing influence awakened the sixteenth century to the movement which has continued down to the present day to engross, and even to create, the energies of philosophic thought in the study of natural phenomena? Obviously some interest was awakened which had before been powerless or had influenced only men of rare and extraordinary genius, or else some opposing interest had ceased to exercise a preponderating influence.

We have now arrived at a new order of inquiries. We ask no longer what are the differences of *method* between ancient and modern scientific researches, but we seek the difference in the *motives* which actuated the philosophic inquiries of the two periods. We seek for the interests which in modern times have so powerfully drawn men of all orders of intelligence to the pursuit of science and to an observance of the conditions requisite for its successful prosecution. This inquiry will, we think, lead to more profitable conclusions than the course we have pursued in review of the theories which have been put forward on this subject. But we have little space in these introductory pages to develop this aspect of the history of science, or to do more than indicate the conclusions we have reached in the classification and history of the dominant motives and the sources of the questions which have determined and directed the pursuit of science. We ask no longer what course has led to successful answers in science but what motives have prompted the pertinent questions.

In place of the positivists' phraseology, that the ancients followed "the subjective method," or appealed for the verification of their theories to natural beliefs, while the moderns follow "the objective method," or appeal to new and independent experimental evidence—if we substitute the word "motive" for "method," we have the terms of one of the conclusions on which we wish to insist. But these require explanation.

By a subjective motive we mean one having its origin in natural universal human interests and emotions, which existed before philosophy was born, which continue to exist in the maturity of philosophy, and determine the character of an important and by no means defunct order of human speculations. By an objective motive we mean one having an empirical origin, arising in the course of an inquiry, springing from interests which are defined by what we already know and not by what we have always felt—interests which depend on acquired knowledge and not on natural desires and emotions. Among the latter we must include the natural desire for knowledge or the primitive, undisciplined sentiment of curiosity. An objective motive is what this becomes when it ceases to be associated with our fears, our respects, our aspirations—our emotional nature; when it ceases to prompt questions as to what relates to our personal destiny, our ambitions, our moral worth; when it ceases to have man, his personal and social nature, as its central and controlling objects. A curiosity which is determined chiefly or solely by the felt imperfections of knowledge as such, and without reference to the uses this knowledge may subserve, is prompted by what we call an objective motive.

A spirit of inquiry which is freed from the influence of our active powers and the interests that gave birth to theological and metaphysical philosophies—which yields passively and easily to the direction of objective motives, to the felt imperfections of knowledge as such—is necessarily, at all times, a weak feeling; and before a body of systematic, well digested, and well ascertained scientific truth had been generated, could hardly have had any persistent influence on the direction of inquiry.

The motives to theological and metaphysical speculation exist from the beginning of civilized human life in the active emotional nature of man. Curiosity as a love of the marvelous or as a love of facts—new facts, prized because they are new and stimulating—also dates back of civilized life. These motives find play in human nature as it emerges from a semianimal state; but they also persist and determine the growth of the human mind in its most advanced development.

The questions of philosophy proper are human desires and fears and aspirations—human emotions—taking an intellectual form. Science follows, but does not supersede, this philosophy. The three phases which the positivists assign to the development of the human mind—the Theological, the Metaphysical, and the Positive or Scientific—are not in reality successive except in their beginnings. They coexist in all the highest developments of civilization and mental activity. They coexisted in the golden age of Greek civilization, in the intense mental activity of the Middle Ages. They move on together in this marvelous modern era. But until this latest epoch positive science was always the inferior philosophy—hardly a distinct philosophy at all—not yet born. But at the beginning of the modern era its gestation was completed. A body of knowledge existed, sufficiently extensive, coherent, and varied, to bear within it a life of its own—an independent life—which was able to collect to itself, by its own determinations, the materials of a continued, new, and ever-increasing mental activity—an activity determined solely by an objective curiosity, or by curiosity in its purest, fullest, and highest energy.

We are probably indebted to the few men of scientific genius who lived during the slow advancement of modern civilization for the foundation of this culture—for the accumulation of the knowledge requisite for this subsequent growth. These men were doubtless, for the most part, the products of their own times and civilization, as indeed all great men have been, but still originators, by concentrating and making productive the energies, tendencies, and knowledges which, but for them, would have remained inert and unfruitful. It is to such men, born at long intervals in the slow progress of civilization, each carrying forward a little the work of his predecessor, that we probably owe our modern science, rather than to the influence of any single mind, like Bacon, who was, like his predecessors, but the lens which collected the light of his times—who prophesied rather than inaugurated the new era. And we owe science to the combined energies of individual men of genius rather than to any tendency to progress inherent in civilization.

We find, then, the explanation of the modern development of science in the accumulation of a body of certified knowledge, sufficiently extensive to engage and discipline a rational scientific curiosity and stimulate it to act independently of other philosophical motives. It is doubtless true that other motives have influenced this development, and especially that motives of material utility have had a powerful effect in stimulating inquiry. Ancient schools of philosophy despised narrow material utilities, the servile arts, and sought no instruction in what moderns dignify by the name of useful arts; but modern science finds in the requirements of the material arts the safest guide to exact knowledge. A theory which is utilized receives the highest possible certificate of truth. Navigation by the aid of astronomical tables, the magnetic telegraph, the innumerable utilities of mechanical and chemical science, are constant and perfect tests of scientific theories, and afford the standard of certitude which science has been able to apply so extensively in its interpretations of natural phenomena. . . .

[HERBERT SPENCER'S USE OF SCIENTIFIC CONCEPTS] [1]

It is certain that the claims of science, as a new power in the world, to the regard of thoughtful and earnest men are receiving a renewed and more candid attention. Through its recent progress, many of the questions which have hitherto remained in the arena of metaphysical disputation are brought forward in new forms and under new auspices. Scientific investigations promise to throw a flood of light on subjects which have interested mankind since the beginning of speculation—subjects related to universal human interests. History, society, laws, and morality—all are claimed as topics with which scien-

[1] [*North American Review*, C (1865), 434-436, 448-460.]

tific methods are competent to deal. Scientific solutions are proposed to all the questions of philosophy which scientific illumination may not show to have their origin in metaphysical hallucination.

Prominent in the ranks of the new school stands Mr. Herbert Spencer,[2] whose versatility has already given to the world many ingenious and original essays in this new philosophy, and whose aspiring genius projects many more, which, if his strength does not fail, are to develop the capacities of a scientific method in dealing with all the problems that ought legitimately to interest the human mind.

The programme of his future labors which his publishers have advertised might dispose a prejudiced critic to look with suspicion on what he has already accomplished; but the favorable impression which his works have made, and the plaudits of an admiring public, demand a suspension of judgment; and the extravagance of his pretensions should for the present be credited to the strength of his enthusiasm.

It is through the past labors of an author that we must judge of his qualifications for future work and the completeness of his preparation. Mr. Spencer's writings evince an extensive knowledge of facts political and scientific, but extensive rather than profound, and all at second hand. It is not, of course, to be expected that a philosopher will be an original investigator in all the departments of knowledge with which he is obliged to have dealings. He must take much at second hand. But original investigations in some department of empirical science are a discipline which best tests and develops even a philosopher's powers. He has in this at least an experience of what is requisite to an adequate comprehension of facts. He learns how to make knowledge profitable to the ascertainment of new truths—an art in which the modern natural philosopher excels. By new

[2] [Herbert Spencer (1820-1903), English philosopher, whose influence on American thought in the latter part of the nineteenth century was enormous. Spencer's famous "law" of evolution—i.e., change from homogeneity to heterogeneity through differentiation and integration—which he applied universally to the movements of nature, was the main target of Wright's criticisms of his so-called scientific philosophy.]

truths must be understood such as are not implied in what we already know, or educible from what is patent to common observation. However skillfully the philosopher may apply his analytical processes to the abstraction of the truths involved in patent facts, the utility of his results will depend not so much on their value and extent as mere abstractions as on their capacity to enlarge our experience by bringing to notice residual phenomena, and making us observe what we have entirely overlooked or search out what has eluded our observation. Such is the character of the principles of modern natural philosophy, both mathematical and physical. They are rather the eyes with which nature is seen than the elements and constituents of the objects discovered. It was in a clear apprehension of this value in the principles of mathematical and experimental science that the excellence of Newton's genius consisted; and it is this value which the Positive Philosophy most prizes. But this is not the value we find in Mr. Spencer's speculations.

Mr. Spencer is not a positivist, though that was not a very culpable mistake which confounded his speculations with the writings of this school. For however much he differs from the positivists in his methods and opinions, he is actuated by the same confidence in the capacities of a scientific method and by the same disrespect for the older philosophies. Mr. Spencer [however] applies a method for the ascertainment of ultimate truths which a positivist would regard as correct only on the supposition that the materials of truth have all been collected and that the research of science is no longer for the enlargement of our experience or for the informing of the mind. Until these conditions be realized, the positivist regards such attempts as Mr. Spencer's as not only faulty, but positively pernicious and misleading. Nothing justifies the development of abstract principles in science but their utility in enlarging our concrete knowledge of nature. The ideas on which mathematical mechanics and the calculus are founded, the morphological ideas of natural history, and the theories of chemistry are such working ideas—finders, not merely summaries of truth. . . .

Judging only by his writings and the general character of

his thinking, we should not ascribe to him that precision in the apprehension of scientific facts which comes chiefly from a successful cultivation of experimental and mathematical research in natural history and natural philosophy. To learn only the results of such researches and the general character of their processes is not enough. One must also be qualified to pursue them. The fact that Mr. Spencer was at one time a civil engineer seems to militate against this judgment of his qualifications. But though a marked success and a reputation acquired in this pursuit would be of great weight in determining our judgment, yet, in the absence of any evidence of this kind, we adhere to the opinion we have formed from his writings. We will say nothing of the impossibility of any one man's acquiring adequately all the knowledge requisite for the successful accomplishment of such an undertaking as Mr. Spencer has proposed for himself.

But a part of this work has become an accomplished fact. The *First Principles* of the new system of philosophy has appeared, and a serial publication of parts of another work on the *Principles of Biology* is now in progress. Mr. Spencer modestly omits from his gigantic scheme any special consideration of physics or the principles of inorganic nature, although his training in mathematics and engineering would seem at first sight to be a preparation best suited to this subject. Perhaps he regards this science as standing in little need of his developments, and besides he has already published some of his views on this subject in his essay on the nebular hypothesis, and his *First Principles* involve generalizations from physical theories.

To the positivists the sciences of general physics, that is astronomy, mechanical and chemical physics, and chemistry, afford the patterns for all the sciences, and some, like physiology, are beginning to profit by such examples. But Mr. Spencer does not find in general physics free play for his ideas. It is only in what constitutes the problems and obscurities of these sciences that he finds free exemplifications of his principles. In the nebular hypothesis and in the obscure relations of physical forces to organic life, and in the hypothesis of the development of organic life through successive geological eras, he is at home. He is conscious of the temptation there is to impose teleological interpretations upon the obscurities of science; and he therefore aims to free his speculations as much as possible from these biases, but with as little success as he had in his *Psychology* in correcting the errors of metaphysics by the light of empirical science.

The idea which has exercised the profoundest influence on the course of Mr. Spencer's thought, as well as on all thought in modern times, and one which appears more or less distinctly in nearly all of Mr. Spencer's writings, is the idea which he elaborates in his *First Principles* as the "Law of Evolution." But what is the origin and value of this idea? Ostensibly it was derived from the investigations of the physiologists in embryology, from Harvey [3] down to the present time. The formula of Von Baer [4] was the first adequate statement of it. This formula Mr. Spencer has elaborated and completed, so as to apply, he thinks, not only to the phenomena of embryology but to the phenomena of nature generally, and especially, as it appears, to those which we know least about, and to those which we only guess at.

But while this is the ostensible origin and scientific value of this idea, its real origin is a very curious and instructive fact in human nature. Progress is a grand idea—Universal Progress is a still grander idea. It strikes the keynote of modern civilization. Moral idealism is the religion of our times. What the ideas God, the One and the All, the Infinite First Cause, were to an earlier civilization, such are Progress and Universal Progress to the modern world—a reflex of its moral ideas and feelings, and not a tradition. Men ever worship the Best, and the consciousness that the Best is attainable is the highest moral conscious-

3 [William Harvey (1578-1657), English physician and anatomist, discovered the circulation of the blood (in the sense of a continuous stream returning to its source).]

4 [Karl Ernst von Baer (1792-1876), German biologist, however, himself accepted the archetypal interpretation of biological species and rejected Darwin's concept of unbroken descent with modification. He did pioneer work in comparative embryology.]

ness, the most inspiring of truths. And when indications of that attainment are visible not merely to the eye of faith but in sensible progress, scientifically measurable, civilization is inspired with a new devotion. Faith that moral perfectibility is possible, not in remote times and places, not in the millennium, not in heaven, but in the furtherance of a present progress, is a faith which to possess in modern times does not make a man suspected of folly or fanaticism. He may forget the past, cease to be religious in the conventional sense of the word, but he is the modern prophet.

When Plato forsook the scientific studies of his youth and found the truest interpretation of nature by asking his own mind what was the best, according to which, he felt sure, the order and framework of nature must be determined, he did but illustrate the influence which strongly impressed moral ideas have on speculative thought at all times; but he did it consciously and avowedly. Modern thinkers may be less conscious of this influence, may endeavor to suppress what consciousness they have of it, warned by the history of philosophy that teleological speculations are exploded follies; nevertheless, the influence surrounds and penetrates them like an atmosphere, unless they be moral phlegmatics and mere lookers-on.

It was Mr. Spencer's aim to free the law of evolution from all teleological implications, and to add such elements and limitations to its definition as should make it universally applicable to the movement of nature. Having done this, as he thinks, he arrives at the following definition: "Evolution is a change from an indefinite incoherent homogeneity to a definite coherent heterogeneity through continuous differentiations and integrations." But teleology is a subtile poison, and lurks where least suspected. The facts of the sciences which Dr. Whewell [5] calls palaetiological, like the various branches of geology, and every actual concrete series of events which together form an

5 [William Whewell (1794-1866), British philosopher and historian of science. For his concept of "palaetiological science," and related notions, cf. his *History of the Inductive Sciences* (1837) and *Philosophy of the Inductive Sciences* (1840).]

object of interest to us, are apt, unless we are fully acquainted with the actual details through observation or by actual particular deductions from well-known particular facts and general laws, to fall into a dramatic procession in our imaginations. The mythic instinct slips into the place of the chronicles at every opportunity. All history is written on dramatic principles. All cosmological speculations are strictly teleological. We never can comprehend the whole of a concrete series of events. What arrests our attention in it is what constitutes the parts of an *order* either real or imaginary, and all merely imaginary orders are dramatic or are determined by interests which are spontaneous in human life. Our speculations about what we have not really observed, to which we supply the order and most of the facts, are necessarily determined by some principle of order in our minds. Now the most general principle which we can have, included by all others, is this: that the concrete series shall be an intelligible series in its entirety, shall only interest and attract our thoughts and a rational curiosity.

But to suppose that such series exist anywhere but where observation and legitimate particular inferences from observation warrant the supposition is to commit the same mistake which has given rise to teleological theories of nature. The "law of causation," the postulate of positive science, does not go to this extent. It does not suppose that there are throughout nature unbroken series in causation, forming in their entirety intelligible wholes, determinable in their beginnings, their progressions, and their ends, with a birth, a growth, a maturation, and a decay. It only presumes that the perhaps unintelligible wholes, both in the sequences and the coexistences of natural phenomena, are composed of intelligible elements; that chaos does not subsist at the heart of things; that the order in nature which is discernible vaguely even to the unobservant implies at least a precise *elementary* order, or fixed relations of antecedents and consequents in its ultimate parts and constituents; that the apparently irregular heterogeneous masses, the concrete series of events, are crystalline in their substance.

To discover these elementary fixed relations of antecedents and consequents is the work of scientific induction; and the only postulate of science is that these relations are everywhere to be found. To account, as far as possible, for any concrete order, like that of life, intelligible as a whole, or regular, is the work of scientific explanation, by deductions from the elementary fixed relations which induction may have discovered. But to explain any such order by simply defining it externally in vague, abstract terms, and to postulate such orders as the components of nature and parts of one complete and intelligible order, is to take a step in advance of legitimate speculation, and a step backward in scientific method—is to commit the mistake of the ancient philosophies of nature.

But Mr. Spencer thinks he has established his "Law of Evolution" by induction. The examples from which he has analyzed his law, the examples of progress in the development of the several elements of civilization, such as languages, laws, fashions, and ideas—the hypothetical examples of the nebular hypothesis and the development hypothesis, and the example of embryological development (the only one our conceptions of which are not liable to be tainted by teleological biases)—are examples which, according to Mr. Spencer's philosophy, afford both the definition and its justification. In other words, his definitions are only carefully elaborated general descriptions in abstract terms; or statements of facts which are observed in numerous instances or classes of instances in terms detached from all objects, in abstract terms, of which the intension is fully known but of which the extension is unknown except through the descriptions they embody. This, though a useful, is a precarious kind of induction, and is apt to lead to premature and false generalizations, or extensions of descriptions to what is hypothetical or unknown. Such inductions are liable to be mistaken for another sort, and to be regarded as not merely general but universal descriptions, and as applicable to what they do not really apply to. This liability is strong just in proportion as prominence is given to such definitions in a philosophical system. No convert to Mr. Spencer's philosophy doubts the substantial correctness of the nebular and development hypotheses, though these are only hypothetical examples of Mr. Spencer's law.

The other sort of inductions to which we have referred are peculiar to the exact inductive sciences. Facts which are not merely general but, from their elementary character and their immediate relations to the orderliness of nature, are presumed to be universal facts are the sort which the positive philosophy most prizes and of which the law of gravitation is the typical example. The honor must be conceded to Mr. Spencer of having elaborated a precise and very abstract description of certain phenomena, the number, the other characters, and the extent of which are, however, unknown, but are all the more imposing from this circumstance.

The law of gravity was a key which deciphered a vast body of otherwise obscure phenomena, and (what is more to the purpose) was successfully applied to the solution of all the problems these phenomena presented. It is common to ascribe to Newton the merit of having discovered the law of gravity in the same sense in which Mr. Spencer may be said to have discovered his law. The justness of this praise may well be doubted, for others had speculated and defined the law of gravity before Newton. What he really discovered was the *universality* of this law, or so nearly discovered it that the astronomers who completed the investigation did not hesitate to concede to him the full honor. He established for it such a degree of probability that his successors pursued the verification with unhesitating confidence, and still pursue it in the fullness of faith.

Mr. Spencer's law is founded on examples, of which only one class, the facts of embryology, are properly scientific. The others are still debated as to their real characters. Theories of society and of the character and origin of social progress, theories on the origins and the changes of organic forms, and theories on the origins and the causes of cosmical bodies and their arrangements, are all liable to the taint of teleological and cosmological conceptions—to spring from the order which the mind imposes upon what it imperfectly observes rather than from that which the objects, were they better known, would supply to the mind.

To us Mr. Spencer's speculation seems but the abstract statement of the cosmological conceptions, and that kind of orderliness which the human mind spontaneously supplies in the absence of facts sufficiently numerous and precise to justify sound scientific conclusions. Progress and development, when they mean more than a continuous proceeding, have a meaning suspiciously like what the moral and mythic instincts are inclined to—something having a beginning, a middle, and an end—an epic poem, a dramatic representation, a story, a cosmogony. It is not sufficient for the purposes of science that the idea of progress be freed from any reference to human happiness as an end. Teleology does not consist entirely of speculations having happy *dénouements,* save that the perfection or the end to which the progress tends is a happiness to the intellect that contemplates it in its evolution and beauty of orderliness. Plato's astronomical speculations were teleological in this artistic sense.

It is not sufficient for the purposes of science that the idea of progress be thus purified; and it would be better if science itself were purified of this idea, at least until proof of its extent and reality be borne in upon the mind by the irresistible force of a truly scientific induction. Aristotle exhibited the characteristics of scientific genius in no way more distinctly than in the rejection of this idea and of all cosmological speculations.

But there is a truth implied in this idea, and an important one—the truth, namely, that the proper objects of scientific research are all of them processes and the results of processes; not the immutable natures which Plato sought for above a world of confusion and unreality, in the world of his own intelligence, but the immutable elements in the orders of all changes, the permanent relations of coexistences and sequences, which are hidden in the confusions of complex phenomena. Thought itself is a process and the mind a complex series of processes, the immutable elements of which must be discovered, not merely by introspection or by self-consciousness, but by the aid of physiological researches and by indirect observation. Everything out of the mind is a product, the result of some process. Nothing is exempt from change. Worlds are formed and dissipated. Races of organic beings grow up like their constituent individual members, and disappear like these. Nothing shows a trace of an original, immutable nature, except the unchangeable laws of change. These point to no beginning and end in time, nor to any bounds in space. All indications to the contrary in the results of physical research are clearly traceable to imperfections in our present knowledge of all the laws of change, and to that disposition to cosmological speculations which still prevails even in science.

We propound these doctrines not as established ones, but as having a warrant from the general results of physical research similar to that which the postulate of science, the law of causation, has in the vaguely discerned order in nature, which forces itself on the attention even of the unobservant. But as a mind unfamiliar with science is easily persuaded that there are phenomena in nature to which the law of causation does not apply, phenomena intrinsically arbitrary and capricious, so even to those most familiar with our present knowledge of physical laws, but who have not attended to the implication of their general characters and relations, the supposition is not incredible that there is a tendency in the forces of nature to a permanent or persistently progressive change in the theater of their operations, and to an ultimate cessation of all the particular conditions on which their manifestations depend. To show why this is incredible to us would carry us beyond the proper limits of our subject, were it not that our author has speculated in the same direction.

Having developed what he thinks to be the true scientific idea of progress in his "Law of Evolution," Mr. Spencer next considers its relations to ultimate scientific ideas, the ideas of space, time, matter, and force. As evolution is change, and as change, scientifically comprehended, is comprehended in terms of matter, motion, and force, and the conditions necessary to these, or time and space, it is necessary that evolution be further defined in its relations to these ideas. These are only formulating terms, entirely abstract. They imply no ontological theory about the nature or existence of mind or matter; and when Mr. Spencer proposes to formulate the phenomena of mind as well as those of matter in terms of matter, motion, and force, it is because these ideas are the only precise ones in which the phenomena of change can be defined.

Mr. Spencer is not a materialist. Materialism and spiritualism, or psychological idealism, are as dogmatic theories equally self-contradictory and absurd. Mr. Spencer is neither a materialist nor an idealist; neither theist, atheist, or pantheist. All these doctrines are, he thinks, without sense or reason; and the philosophers who invented them, and the disciples who received and thought they understood them, were deceived. But we are inclined to the opinion that believers, though they may be deceived about their ability to comprehend these theories (for it is easy to mistake meanings), are not deceived about the motives or the spirit which prompts these speculations, and which in fact determines for each his election of what doctrine best suits his character. For within the pale of philosophy, character determines belief, and ideas stand for feelings. We receive the truths of science on compulsion. Nothing but ignorance is able to resist them. In philosophy we are free from every bias except that of our own characters; and it therefore seems to us becoming in a philosopher, who is solicitous about the moral reputation of his doctrines, who would avoid classification under disreputable categories, that he teach nothing which he does not know, lest the direction of his inquiries be mistaken for that of his dispositions. The vulgar who use these obnoxious terms, materialism, atheism, pantheism, do not pretend to define them; but they somehow have a very definite idea, or at least a strong feeling, about the dangerous character of such speculations, which are none the less reprehensible because inconceivable.

But we must defer the consideration of the moral character of Mr. Spencer's speculations until we have further examined their scientific grounds.

Terms which the real physicist knows how to use as the terms of mathematical formulas and which were never even suspected of any heterodox tendencies, terms which have been of inestimable service both in formulating and finding out the secrets of nature, are appropriated by Mr. Spencer to the further elaboration of his vague definitions, and to the abstract description of as much in real nature as they may happen to apply to. As if an inventory of the tools of any craft were a proper account of its handiwork! Out of mathematical formulas these terms lose their definiteness and their utility. They become corrupting and misleading ideas. They are none the less abstract, but they are less clear. They again clothe themselves in circumstance, though vaguely. They appeal to that indefinite consciousness which, as Mr. Spencer says, cannot be formulated, but in which he thinks we have an apprehension of cause and causal agencies.

> "Though along with the extension of generalizations, and concomitant integrations of conceived causal agencies," says Mr. Spencer, "the conceptions of causal agencies grow more indefinite; and though as they gradually coalesce into a universal causal agency they cease to be representable in thought, and are no longer supposed to be comprehensible, yet the consciousness of *cause* remains as dominant to the last as it was at first, and can never be got rid of. The consciousness of cause can be abolished only by abolishing consciousness itself."

This is quoted by himself from his *First Principles* as one of his "reasons for dissenting from the philosophy of M. Comte." Though he seems solicitous to avoid all ontological implications in his use of scientific terms, yet we cannot avoid the impression of a vague metaphysical signification in his speculations, as if he were presenting all the parts of a system of materialism except the affirmative and negative copulas. These are withheld, because we cannot be supposed to believe anything inconceivable, as all ontological dogmas are. He seems to lead us on to the point of requiring our assent to a materialistic doctrine and then lets us off on account of the infirmities of our minds, presenting materialism to our contemplation rather than to our understanding.

Mr. Spencer regards the ultimate ideas of science as unknowable; and in a sense the meanings of the abstractest terms are unknowable, that is, are not referable to any notions more abstract nor susceptible of sensuous apprehension or representation as such. But the way to know them is to use them in mathematical formulas to express precisely what we do know. It is true that this cannot yet be done, except in the physical sciences proper, and not always with distinctness in these. It is only in astronomy and mechanical physics that these terms are used with mathematical precision. They change their meanings, or at least lose their definiteness, when we come to chemistry and physiology.

"The indestructibility of matter," "the continuity of motion," "the conservation of force," and "the correlation and equivalence of forces" are ideas which mathematical and physical science has rendered familiar. Besides these, Mr. Spencer has analyzed others, descriptive of the general external characteristics of motion; and he continues with a development of what the Law of Evolution implies. To all the ideas which he adopts from science he adds a new sense, or rather a vagueness, so as to make them descriptive of as much as possible. One of these ideas loses in the process so many of its original features, as well as its name, that we should not have recognized it as the same but for Mr. Spencer's justification of what he regards as a change of nomenclature. He prefers "persistence of force" to "conservation of force," because the latter "implies a conservator and an act of conserving,"and because "it does not imply the existence of the force before that particular manifestation of it with which we commence." Science, we are inclined to believe, will not adopt this emendation, because the conservation it refers to is that whereby the special conditions of the production of any mechanical effect in nature are themselves replaced by the changes through which this effect is manifested; so that if this effect ceases to appear as a motion, it nevertheless exists in the altered antecedents of motions, which may subsequently be developed in the course of natural changes. It is this conservation of the conditions of motion by the operations of nature through the strictest observation of certain mathematical laws that science wishes to express. The objection (if there be any) to this phrase is in the word "force." This word is used in mathematical mechanics in three different senses, but fortunately they are distinct. They are not here fused together, as they are by Mr. Spencer, into one vague expression of what nobody in fact knows anything about. There is no danger of ambiguities arising from this source in mathematics. The ideas expressed by this word are perfectly distinct and definable. The liability to ambiguity is only when we pass from mathematical formulas to sciences, in which the word has more or less of vagueness and an ontological reference. This liability is somewhat diminished, at least so far as distinct mathematical comprehension is concerned, by the use of the phrases "conservation of mechanical effect" or "the law of power," which are now employed to express the mathematical theorem which has as one of its corollaries the doctrine that "perpetual motion" is impossible in the sense in which practical mechanics use the words. This theorem is deduced from the fundamental laws of motion, or those transcendental ideas and definitions which have received their proof or justification in their ability to clear up the confusions with which the movements of nature fall upon the senses and present themselves to the undisciplined understanding.

The phrase "conservation of force" was adopted from mathematical mechanics into chemical physics, with reference to the question of the possibility of "perpetual motion" by means of those natural forces with which chemistry deals. The impossibility of "perpetual motion," or the fact that "in the series of natural processes there is no circuit to be found by which mechanical force can be gained without a corresponding consumption," had been demonstrated only with reference to the so-called "fixed forces" of nature, or those which depend solely on the relative distances of bodies from each other. Chemical forces are not mathematically comprehended, and are therefore utterly unknown, save in their effects, and their laws are unknown, save in the observed invariable orders of these effects. These forces are merely hypotheses, and hypotheses which include little or nothing that is definite or profitable to research. But mechanical forces suggested to physicists a problem perfectly clear and definite. "Are the laws of chemical forces also inconsistent with 'perpetual motion'?" "Are light, heat, electricity, magnetism, and the force of chemical transformations correlated with each other and with mechanical motions and forces as these are among themselves?" Here is something tangible; and the direction which these questions have given to physical researches in recent times mark out a distinct epoch in scientific progress. Here the answer could not be found a priori, as a consequent of any known or presumed universal laws of nature. Experiment must establish these presumptions; and it does so with such an overwhelming amount of evidence that they are made the grounds of prediction, as the law of gravity was in the discovery of the planet Uranus. Physicists have anticipated, on the ground of the impossibility of perpetual motion, such an apparently remote fact as this, "that the freezing temperature in water depends on the pressure to which the water is subjected." Experiment confirms this anticipation.

The processes of such researches are long and intricate, but they are perfectly precise and definite; and it is thus that the law of the "Conservation of Force" is made of value, and not by such use as Mr. Spencer is able to make of it, if indeed his "Persistence of Force" can be regarded as having any meaning in common with it. His principle seems to us to bear a much closer resemblance to the old metaphysical "Principle of Causality," or the impossibility of any change in the quantity of existence (whatever this may mean); and it also seems to us to be as profitless. . . .

[THE LOGIC OF EVOLUTIONARY THEORY]

[I. Evolution and Its Explanation] [1]

It is now nearly twelve years since the discussion of that "mystery of mysteries," the origin of species, was reopened by the publication of the first edition of Mr. Darwin's most remarkable work. Again and again in the history of scientific debate this question had been discussed, and, after exciting a short-lived interest, had been condemned by cautious and conservative thinkers to the limbo of insoluble problems or to the realm of religious mystery. They had, therefore, sufficient grounds, a priori, for anticipating that a similar fate would attend this new revival of the question and that, in a few years, no more would be heard of the matter; that the same condemnation awaited this movement which had overwhelmed the venturesome speculations of Lamarck [2] and of the author of the *Vestiges of Creation*.[3] This not unnatural anticipation has been, however, most signally disappointed. Every year has increased the interest felt in the question, and at the present moment the list of publications which we place at the head of this article [4] testifies to the firm hold which the subject has acquired in this short period on the speculative interests of all inquisitive minds. But what can we say has really been accomplished by this debate; and what reasons have we for believing that the judgment of conservative thinkers will not, in the main, be proved right after

1 [*North American Review*, CXIII (1871), 63-66.]

2 [Lamarck, Jean De Monet, Chevalier de (1744-1829), French naturalist, believed, like Buffon before him, that species were not unalterable but that the more complex developed from pre-existent simpler forms. Lamarck, of course, is best known for his belief that acquired characteristics are inherited.]

3 [Published anonymously in 1845. Its author was Robert Chambers.]

4 [Darwin's *The Descent of Man* and the fifth edition of his *On the Origin of Species;* Alfred Russel Wallace's *Contributions to the Theory of Natural Selection;* and St. George Mivart's *On the Genesis of Species.*]

all, though present indications are against them? One permanent consequence, at least, will remain, in the great additions to our knowledge of natural history and of general physiology or theoretical biology which the discussion has produced, though the greater part of this positive contribution to science is still to be credited directly to Mr. Darwin's works, and even to his original researches. But, besides this, an advantage has been gained which cannot be too highly estimated. Orthodoxy has been won over to the doctrine of evolution. In asserting this result, however, we are obliged to make what will appear to many persons important qualifications and explanations. We do not mean that the heads of leading religious bodies, even in the most enlightened communities, are yet willing to withdraw the dogma that the origin of species is a special religious mystery, or even to assent to the hypothesis of evolution as a legitimate question for scientific inquiry. We mean only that many eminent students of science, who claim to be orthodox and who are certainly actuated as much by a spirit of reverence as by scientific inquisitiveness, have found means of reconciling the general doctrine of evolution with the dogmas they regard as essential to religion. Even to those whose interest in the question is mainly scientific this result is a welcome one, as opening the way for a freer discussion of subordinate questions, less trammeled by the religious prejudices which have so often been serious obstacles to the progress of scientific researches.

But again, in congratulating ourselves on this result, we are obliged to limit it to the doctrine of evolution in its most general form, the theory common to Lamarck's zoological philosophy, to the views of the author of the *Vestiges of Creation,* to the general conclusions of Mr. Darwin's and Mr. Wallace's [5]

[5] [Alfred Russel Wallace (1823-1913), British naturalist, along with Darwin, offered the concept of natural selection as an explanation for descent with modification. The simple description "descent with modification" is that most general form of evolutionary theory to which Wright refers. Unlike Darwin, however, Wallace denied that man, like other animals, had been produced by the unaided operation of natural selection. Wright's *Evolution of Self-Consciousness* was written as a direct challenge to Wallace's restriction of the operation of natural selection.]

theory of natural selection, to Mr. Spencer's general doctrine of evolution, and to a number of minor explanations of the processes by which races of animals and plants have been derived by descent from different ancestral forms. What is no longer regarded with suspicion as secretly hostile to religious beliefs by many truly religious thinkers is that which is denoted in common by the various names "transmutation," "development," "derivation," "evolution," and "descent with modification." These terms are synonymous in their primary and general signification, but refer secondarily to various hypotheses of the processes of derivation. But there is a choice among them on historical grounds, and with reference to associations, which are of some importance from a theological point of view. "Transmutation" and "development" are under ban. "Derivation" is, perhaps, the most innocent word; though "evolution" will probably prevail, since, in spite of its etymological implication, it has lately become most acceptable, not only to the theological critics of the theory, but to its scientific advocates; although, from the neutral ground of experimental science, "descent with modification" is the most pertinent and least exceptionable name.

While the general doctrine of evolution has thus been successfully redeemed from theological condemnation, this is not yet true of the subordinate hypothesis of natural selection, to the partial success of which this change of opinion is, in great measure, due. It is, at first sight, a paradox that the views most peculiar to the eminent naturalist whose work has been chiefly instrumental in effecting this change of opinion should still be rejected or regarded with suspicion by those who have nevertheless been led by him to adopt the general hypothesis—an hypothesis which his explanations have done so much to render credible. It would seem, at first sight, that Mr. Darwin has won a victory, not for himself, but for Lamarck. Transmutation, it would seem, has been accepted, but natural selection, its explanation, is still rejected by many converts to the general theory, both on religious and scientific grounds. But too much weight might easily be attributed to the deductive or explanatory part of the evidence, on which the doctrine of evolution has come to rest. In the half-century preceding the publication of the *Origin of Species,* inductive evidence on the subject had accumulated greatly outweighing all that was previously known; and the *Origin of Species* is not less remarkable as a compend and discussion of this evidence than for the ingenuity of its explanations. It is not, therefore, to what is now known as "Darwinism" that the prevalence of the doctrine of evolution is to be attributed, or only indirectly. Still, most of this effect is due to Mr. Darwin's work, and something undoubtedly to the indirect influence of reasonings that are regarded with distrust by those who accept their conclusions; for opinions are contagious, even where their reasons are resisted. . . .

[II. The Logic of Biology] [6]

General physiology, or physical and theoretical biology, are sciences in which, through the study of the laws of inheritance and the direct and indirect effect of external conditions, we must arrive, if in any way, at a more and more definite knowledge of the causes of specific manifestations; and this is what Mr. Darwin's labors have undertaken to do, and have partially accomplished. Every step he has taken has been in strict conformity to the principles of method which the examples of inductive and experimental science have established. . . . The "realism" of ascribing efficacy to an abstraction vitiates nearly all speculations in theoretical biology which are not designedly, or even instinctively, as in Mr. Darwin's work, made to conform to the rigorous rules of experimental philosophy. These require us to assume no causes that are not true or phenomenally known, and known in some other way than in the effect to be explained; and to prove the sufficiency of those we do assume in some other way than by putting an abstract name or description of an effect for its cause, like using the words "attraction" and "polarity" to account for things the matters of which have *come to-*

[6] [*North American Review,* CXIII (1871), 72-75; CXV (1872), 22-24.]

gether in a *definite form.* It may seem strange to many readers to be told that Mr. Darwin, the most consummate speculative genius of our times, is no more a maker of hypotheses than Newton was, who, unable to discover the cause of the properties of gravitation, wrote the often-quoted but much misunderstood words, *Hypotheses non fingo.* "For," he adds, "whatever is not deduced from the phenomena is to be called an hypothesis; and hypotheses, whether metaphysical or physical, whether of occult qualities or mechanical, have no place in experimental philosophy. In this philosophy particular propositions are inferred from the phenomena, and afterwards rendered general by induction. Thus it was that the impenetrability, the mobility, and the impulsive force of bodies, and the laws of motion and gravitation, were discovered. And to us it is enough that gravity does really exist and act according to the laws which we have explained, and abundantly serves to account for all the motions of the celestial bodies and of our sea." Thus, also, it is that the variability of organisms and the known laws of variation and inheritance, and of the influence of external conditions, and the law of natural selection, have been discovered. And though it is not enough that variability and selection do really exist and act according to laws which Mr. Darwin has explained (since the limits of their action and efficiency are still to be ascertained), yet it is enough for the present that Darwinians do not rest, like their opponents, contented with framing what Newton would have called, if he had lived after Kant, "transcendental hypotheses," which have no place in experimental philosophy. It may be said that Mr. Darwin has invented the hypothesis of pangenesis against the rules of this philosophy; but so also did Newton invent the corpuscular theory of light, with a similar purpose and utility.

In determining the limits of the action of natural selection, and its sufficiency within these limits, the same demonstrative adequacy should not, for obvious reasons, be demanded as conditions of assenting to its highly probable truth that Newton proved for his speculation. For the facts for this investigation are hopelessly wanting. Astronomy presents the anomaly, among the physical sciences, of being the only science that deals in the concrete with a few naturally isolated causes, which are separated from all other lines of causation in a way that in other physical sciences can only be imitated in the carefully guarded experiments of physical and chemical laboratories. The study of animals and plants under domestication is, indeed, a similar mode of isolating with a view to ascertaining the physical laws of life by inductive investigations. But the theory of natural selection, in its actual application to the phenomena of life and the origin of species, should not be compared to the theory of gravitation in astronomy, nor to the principles of physical science as they appear in the natures that are shut in by the experimental resources of the laboratory, but rather to these principles as they are actually working, and have been working, in the concrete courses of outward nature, in meteorology and physical geology. Still better, perhaps, at least for the purposes of illustration, we may compare the principle of natural selection to the fundamental laws of political economy, demonstrated and actually at work in the production of the values and the prices in the market of the wealth which human needs and efforts demand and supply. Who can tell from these principles what the market will be next week, or account for its prices of last week, even by the most ingenious use of hypotheses to supply the missing evidence? The empirical economist and statistician imagines that he can discover some other principles at work, some predetermined regularity in the market, some "innate" principles in it, to which the general laws of political economy are subordinated; and speculating on them, might risk his own wealth in trade, as the speculative "vitalist" might, if anything could be staked on a transcendental hypothesis. In the same way the empirical weather-philosopher thinks he can discern regularities in the weather which the known principles of mechanical and chemical physics will not account for and to which they are subordinate. This arises chiefly from his want of imagination, of a clear mental grasp of these principles, and of an adequate knowledge of the resources of legitimate hypothesis to supply the place of the unknown incidental causes through which these principles act. Such are also the sources of most of the difficulties which [Mr. Mivart[7]] has found in the applications of the theory of natural selection. . . . It was a part of Mr. Mivart's plan, in attacking the hypothesis of the predominant agency of natural selection in the origination of species, to discredit a number of such subordinate hypotheses [what may be called hypotheses of the second degree, or the discussion of hypothetical illustrations of the action of natural selection], as well as challenge the theory to offer any adequate ones for the explanation of certain extraordinary structures. We considered in detail several objections of this sort, though we might have been content with simply pointing out a sufficient answer in the logical weakness of such a mode of attack. The illustrations of the theory which have been proposed have in general not at all the force of arguments, or except where the utility of a structure is simple and obvious and can be shown by direct evidence to be effective in developing it out of accidental beginnings, and even in perfecting it, as in cases of the mimicry of certain insects by others for a protection, which is thus really acquired. In general, such illustrations serve only to show the mode of action supposed in the theory without pretending to reconstruct the past history of an animal, even by the roughest sketch; or to determine all the uses, or the relative importance of them, in any structure. To discredit these particular secondary hypotheses has no more weight as an argument against the theory than the hypotheses themselves have in confirmation of it. To be convinced on general grounds that such a structure as that of the giraffe's neck was developed by insensible steps from a more common form of the neck in ungulates, through the oscillations of individual differences, and by the special utilities of the variations which have made the neck longer in some individuals than in others, or through the utilities of these to the animals under the special conditions of their past existence, is

[7] [St. George Mivart (1827-1900), English biologist, wrote his *Genesis of Species,* the book to which Wright here refers, in 1871. Mivart was a naturalist who accepted the concept of evolution but rejected Darwin's explanation of it in terms of natural selection.]

very different from believing that this or that particular use in the structure was *the* utility (to adopt our author's favorite form of definiteness) which governed the selection or determined the survival of the fittest. *The* use which may be presumed in general to govern selection is a combination, with various degrees of importance, of all the actual uses in a structure. There can be no more propriety in demanding of the theory of natural selection that it should define this use, or trace out the history hypothetically of any particular structure in its relations to past conditions of existence, than there would be in demanding of political economy that it should justify the correctness of its general principles by success in explaining the record of past prices in detail, or accounting in particular for a given financial anomaly. In either case, the proper evidence is wanting. Any instance of a structure which could be conclusively shown (a very difficult kind of proof) to exist, or to be developed in any way, without reference in the process of development to any utility whatever, past or present, or to any past forms of the structure, would be an instance in point, and would go far toward qualifying the evidence, otherwise mostly affirmative, of the predominant agency of natural selection.

We may remark by the way that Mr. Mivart's definite thesis, "that natural selection is not *the* origin of species," is really not *the* question. No more was ever claimed for it than that it is the most influential of the agencies through which species have been modified. Lamarck's principle of the direct effect of habit, or actual use and disuse, has never been abandoned by later evolutionists; and Mr. Darwin has given much more space to its proof and illustration in his work on *Variation under Domestication* than any other writer. Moreover the physiological causes which produce reversions and correlations of growth, and which, so far as they are known, are quite independent of natural selection, are also assigned as causes of change. But all these are subordinated in the theory to the advantage and consequent survival of the fittest in the struggle for life, or to natural selection. Upon this point we must refer our readers to the "additions and corrections" in the lately published sixth edition of the *Origin of Species;* in which also all the objections brought forward by Mr. Mivart, which had not previously been examined in the work, are fully considered; and, we need hardly add, far more thoroughly and adequately than could be possible for us, or in the pages of this Review. . . .

[III. The Meaning of "Accident"] [8]

The almost universal prevalence of well-marked phenomena of variation in species, the absolutely universal fact that no two individual organisms are exactly alike, and that the description of a species is necessarily abstract and in many respects by means of averages—these facts have received no particular explanations, and might indeed be taken as ultimate facts or highest laws in themselves, were it not that in biological speculations such an assumption would be likely to be misunderstood, as denying the existence of any real determining causes and more ultimate laws, as well as denying any known antecedents or regularities in such phenomena. No physical naturalist would for a moment be liable to such a misunderstanding, but would, on the contrary, be more likely to be off his guard against the possibility of it in minds otherwise trained and habituated to a different kind of studies. Mr. Darwin has undoubtedly erred in this respect. He has not in his works repeated with sufficient frequency his faith in the universality of the law of causation in the phenomena of general physiology or theoretical biology as well as in all the rest of physical nature. He has not said often enough, it would appear, that in referring any effect to "accident," he only means that its causes are like particular phases of the weather, or like innumerable phenomena in the concrete course of nature generally, which are quite beyond the power of finite minds to anticipate or to account for in detail, though none the less really determinate or due to regular causes. That he has committed this error appears from the fact that his critic, Mr. Mivart, has made the mistake, which

[8] [*North American Review,* CXIII (1871), 67-69, 78, 80-81.]

nullifies nearly the whole of his criticism, of supposing that "the theory of Natural Selection may (though it need not) be taken in such a way as to lead men to regard the present organic world as formed, so to speak, *accidentally,* beautiful and wonderful as is confessedly the hap-hazard result" (p. 33). Mr. Mivart, like many another writer, seems to forget the age of the world in which he lives and for which he writes—the age of "experimental philosophy," the very standpoint of which, its fundamental assumption, is the universality of physical causation. This is so familiar to minds bred in physical studies that they rarely imagine that they may be mistaken for disciples of Democritus, or for believers in "the fortuitous concourse of atoms," in the sense, at least, which theology has attached to this phrase. If they assent to the truth that may have been meant by the phrase, they would not for a moment suppose that the atoms move fortuitously but only that their conjunctions, constituting the actual concrete orders of events, could not be anticipated except by a knowledge of the natures and regular histories of each and all of them—such knowledge as belongs only to omniscience. The very hope of experimental philosophy, its expectation of constructing the sciences into a true philosophy of nature, is based on the induction, or, if you please, the a priori presumption, that physical causation is universal; that the constitution of nature is written in its actual manifestations, and needs only to be deciphered by experimental and inductive research; that it is not a latent invisible writing, to be brought out by the magic of mental anticipation or metaphysical meditation. Or, as Bacon said, it is not by the "anticipations of the mind" but by the "interpretation of nature" that natural philosophy is to be constituted; and this is to presume that the order of nature is decipherable, or that causation is everywhere either manifest or hidden but never absent. . . .

The accidental causes of science are only "accidents" relatively to the intelligence of a man. Eclipses have the least of this character to the astronomer of all the phenomena of nature; yet to the savage they are the most terrible of monstrous accidents. The accidents of monstrous variation, or even of the small and limited variations normal in any race or species, are only accidents relatively to the intelligence of the naturalist, or to his knowledge of general physiology. An accident is what cannot be anticipated from what we know, or by any intelligence, perhaps, which is less than omniscient. . . .

[Moreover,] the class of variations, that is, "individual differences," constant and normal in a race, but having different ranges in different races, or in the same race under different circumstances, may be regarded as in no proper sense accidentally related to the advantages that come from them; or in no other sense than a tendril, or a tentacle, or a hand searching in the dark, is accidentally related to the object it succeeds in finding. And yet we say properly that it was by "accident" that a certain tendril was put forth so as to fulfill its function and clasp the particular object by which it supports the vine; or that it was an accidental movement of the tentacle or hand that brought the object it has secured within its grasp. The search was, and continues to be, normal and general; it is the particular success only that is accidental; and this only in the sense that lines of causation, stretching backward infinitely, and unrelated except in a first cause, or in the total order of nature, come together and by their concurrence produce it. Yet over even this concurrence "law" still presides, to the effect that for every such concurrence the same consequences follow. . . .

[IV. Real or Conventional Species] [9]

The question of zoological philosophy, "Whether species have a real existence in nature," in the decision of which naturalists have so generally agreed with Linnaeus,[10] refers directly and explicitly to the question of the fixity of essential characters, and to the assumption that species must remain un-

[9] [*North American Review*, CXV (1872), 16-19.]

[10] [Linnaeus [Carl von Linné] (1707-1778), Swedish botanist, first enunciated the principles for classifying plants and animals according to genera and species and adhered to a uniform use of specific names. Cf. R. Pulteney's *General View of the Writings of Linnaeus* (1781).]

altered in these respects so long as they continue to exist, or until they give birth to new species—or, as was formerly believed, give place in perishing to new independent creations. The distinction involved in this question should not be confounded, as it might easily be, with the distinction in logic of "real kinds" from other class names. Logic recognizes a principal division in class names, according as these are the names of objects which agree with each other and differ from other objects in a very large and indefinite number of particulars or attributes, or are the names of objects which agree only in a few and a definite number of attributes. The former are the names of "real kinds," and include the names of natural species, as man, horse, etc., and of natural genera, as whale, oak, etc. These classes are "real kinds," not because the innumerable particulars in which the individual members of them agree with each other and differ from the members of other classes, are themselves fixed or invariable in time, but because this sort of agreement and difference is fixed or continues to appear. An individual hipparion resembled its immediate parents and the other offspring of them as closely as, or, at least, in the same intimate manner in which one horse resembles another, namely, in innumerable details. But this is not opposed to the conception that the horse is descended from the hipparion by insensible steps of gradation or continuously. For examples of names that are not the names of "real kinds," we may instance such objects as those that are an inch in length, or in breadth, or are colored black, or are square, or (combining these particulars) such objects as black square inches. These may be made of paper, or wood, or ivory, or differ in all other respects except the enumerated and definite particulars. They are not "real" or natural "kinds," but factitious ones.

The confusion which, as we have said, might arise between the "real kinds" of logic and the *real* species of biological speculation would depend on a vagueness in the significance of the word "real," which in common usage combines in uncertain proportions two elementary and more precise ideas, that of fixedness and that of breadth of relationship. Both these marks of reality are applied habitually as tests of it. Thus if an object attests its existence to several of my senses, is seen, heard, touched, and varied in its relations to these senses, and moreover is similarly related to the senses of another person, as evinced by his testimony, then I know that the object is real, and not a mere hallucination or invention of my fantasy; though it may disappear immediately afterwards in an unexplained manner, or be removed by some unknown but supposable agency. Here the judgment of reality depends on breadth of relationship to my experience and sources of knowledge. Or again I may only *see* the object, and consult no other eyes than my own; but seeing it often, day after day, in the same place, I shall judge it a real object, provided its existence is conformable to the general possibilities of experience, or to the test of "breadth." Here the test of reality is "fixity" or continuance in time. That natural species are real in one of these senses, or that individuals of a species are alike in an indefinite number of particulars or resemble each other intimately, is unquestionable as a fact, and is not an invention of the understanding or classifying faculty, and is moreover the direct natural consequence of the principles of inheritance. In this sense species are equivalent to large natural stocks or races existing for a limited but indeterminate number of generations. That they are real in the other sense, or fixed in time absolutely in respect to any of the particulars of their resemblance, whether these are essential (that is, useful for discrimination and classification) or are not, is far from being the axiom it has seemed to be. It is, on the contrary, highly improbable, though tacitly assumed, as we have seen, in criticisms of the theory of natural selection; and in that significance often attached to the word "species" in which the notions of fixedness and distinctiveness have coalesced. It is true that without this significance in the word "species" the names and descriptions of organic forms could not be permanently applicable. No system of classification, however natural or real, could be final. Classification would, indeed, be wholly inadequate as a representation of the organic world on the whole, or as a sketch of the "plan of creation," and would be falsely conceived as revealing the categories and thoughts of creative intelligence—a consequence by no means welcome to the devout naturalist, since it seems to degrade the value of his work. But this may be because he has misconceived its true value, and dedicated to the science of divinity what is really the rightful inheritance of natural or physical science.

If instead of implicitly assuming the principle of specific stability in the criticisms of the earlier chapters of his book, and deferring the explicit consideration of it to a later chapter and as a special topic, [Mr. Mivart] had undertaken the establishment of it as the essential basis of his theory (as indeed it really is), he would have attacked the theory of natural selection in a most vital point; and if he had succeeded, all further criticism of the theory would have been superfluous. But without success in establishing this essential basis, he leaves his own theory and his general difficulties on the theory of natural selection without adequate foundation. The importance of natural selection in the evolution of organic species (its predominant influence) depends entirely on the truth of the opposite assumption, the *instability* of species. The evidences for and against this position are various, and are not adequately considered in the author's chapter on this subject. Moreover, some of the evidences may be expected to be greatly affected by what will doubtless be the discoveries of the immediate future. Already the difficulties of discrimination and classification in dealing with large collections have become very great in some departments of natural history, and even in paleontology the gradations of fossil forms are becoming finer and finer with almost every new discovery; and this in spite of the fact that nothing at all approaching to evidence of continuity can rationally be expected anywhere from the fragmentary geological record. To this evidence must be added the phenomena of variation under domestication. The apparent limits of the changes which can be effected by artificial selection are not, as they have been thought, proofs of the doctrine of "specific stability," or of the opinion of Linnaeus, but only indications of the dependence of variation on physiological causes and on laws of inheritance; and also of the fact that the laws of variation and the action of natural selection are not suspended by domestication but may oppose the aims and efforts of artificial selection. The real point of the proof afforded by these phenomena is that permanent changes may be effected in species by insensible degrees. They are permanent, however, only in the sense that no tendency to reversion will restore the original form, except by the action of similar causes. . . .

II

RELIGIOUS AND MORAL PHILOSOPHY

To Mr. F. E. Abbot [1]

Cambridge, Oct. 28, 1867.

You ask to be admitted to my confidence by learning from me my speculative beliefs concerning the existence of a God and the immortality of the soul, and promise not to be shocked by any revelations I may make. The verdict of "not proven" is the kind of judgment I have formed on these matters; but not on that account am I warranted in taking up a position against the general opinion of my fellow citizens, for this would be to become as illogical as the most confident among them. Atheism is speculatively as unfounded as theism, and practically can only spring from bad motives. I mean, of course, dogmatic atheism. A *bigoted* atheist seems to me the meanest and narrowest of men. In fact, practical considerations determine that a state of suspended judgment on these themes is the state of stable equilibrium. I have no desire to wake into a strange, unknown future life, and I can discover no valid reasons for any confidence in such a waking. As purely speculative or scientific doctrines, these demand assent no more cogently than a theory that some distant planet is inhabited, or, better still, that the planet is largely composed of granite or some other stated substance—for we might have a sentimental bias in favor of an inhabited planet.

Practical grounds are really the basis of belief in the doctrines of theology. The higher moral sentiments have attached themselves so strongly to these traditions that doubts of them seem to the believers like contempt for all that is noble or worthy in

[1] [*Letters*, pp. 133-135.]

human character. This paralogism even goes so far as to declare man's life utterly worthless, unless it is to be prolonged to infinity; that is, I suppose, the worth of any part—say a year's life—is infinitesimal, even if filled with the purest enjoyments, the noblest sympathies, and the most beneficent activities. In whichever conclusion respecting a future life I might seek at last to cease from questioning and to willfully resolve my doubts, I should never cease to repudiate such a view of the value of the present human life.

You perceive that on practical grounds I openly dissent from orthodoxy, but I may appear to you to evade the speculative questions. I do not think that I do; for though I may not consistently hold on all occasions the even balance of judgment and the open mind which I think as proper in such matters as in all others, it is at any rate my design to do so. Whichever way we yield assent, we feel ourselves carried, not by evidence, but by the prejudices of feeling. We fall into one or another form of superstitious belief. Suspension of judgment appears to me to be demanded, therefore, not merely by the evidence, but as a discipline of character—that faith and moral effort may not waste themselves on idle dreams but work among the realities of life. Practical theism, if it means, as it ordinarily does, the exclusion from the mind of all evidence not favorable to received religious doctrines, seems to me to put religious sentiment in a false position—one incompatible, not only with intellectual freedom, but with the soundest development of religious character—with that unreserved devotion to the best *we know,* which tries all things, and holds fast to that which is good.

Very few men could confess a belief in a God or a disbelief in one without expressing more than their speculative convictions. So far from being like their opinions on the law of gravitation, it would almost necessarily be with feelings of exultation, enthusiasm, and hope, or with bitterness, contempt, or despair—so strong are the associations of feeling attached to this word. Nevertheless, it is a doctrine of positivism that the real interests of moral and religious culture, no less than those of scientific knowledge, are quite independent in fact (and might be made so in education) of these doctrines and associations. And this is also my belief.

I sincerely regret to learn from you that your views have brought you into such difficulties as to render it necessary to give up your profession [ministry]. Would teaching private pupils, fitting boys for college, be an employment you would like? It is one of the most remunerative to those who are in the way to get it; and, although I am not in that way, I think it would not be difficult to find such employment. I should be happy to use all my influence to this end. I am told that there is a good opportunity at present to start a school for young ladies in Boston; for, though there are several excellent schools kept by ladies, there are none equal to Professor Torrey's, which he gave up when he came to Cambridge.

But I hope that I have misunderstood you, and that you will be able to continue, as a religious instructor, to exemplify how irrelevant metaphysics really are to the clergyman's true influence—quite as much so, I think, as to that of the scientific teacher. The pursuit of philosophy ought to be a side study. Nothing so much justifies that shameful assumption by ecclesiastical bodies of control over speculative opinions as the inconsiderate preaching of such opinions, in place of the warnings, encouragements, sympathies, and persuasions of the true religious instructor. The lessons which he has to deliver are really very easy to understand but hard to live up to. To help to live up to the true ideals of life seems to me the noblest, if not the only, duty of the preacher.

To Mr. Abbot.[2]

Cambridge, Feb. 10, 1869.

I have had the proposition [3] of your letter of so long ago so long in debate that I presume you have concluded ere this that

[2] [*Letters,* pp. 140-142.]

[3] [A request that Wright contribute an article on "The Religious Aspects of Positivism" to a volume which Abbot proposed to publish.]

my silence means dissent. This I am now persuaded is the true interpretation, though contrary to the current maxim.

I owe you an apology for this delay in answering your kind letter, to which you wished an immediate reply. But I really desired to see my way clear to meeting your wishes and my own, touching the essay on the positivists' religion; and I regret very much that I cannot count upon myself as good for so difficult and delicate a task. My pen has of late forsaken the paths of speculation, and I have not been able to persuade it back.

I do not feel competent, nor do I care, to address, unprovoked, a large promiscuous audience, the majority of whom judge by texts and phrases, and apply the touchstone of magical words—and so think they think. Something more stimulating, like misrepresentation by an opponent, or like personal debate, must inspire me. A cold thesis, served in a book, does not incite the speculative appetite with me; and I confess to the heartiest sympathy with Plato's preference for a *man*, who can question and answer, rather than for a book, which must say much at random, or demand an artist's skill and imagination in the writer. One of the most important of the teacher's or preacher's qualifications, yet one of the rarest, is a knowledge of the hearer's mind, so that his discourse may answer to something, or else raise clear and profitable questions. Most philosophical books, lectures, and sermons seem to me either mechanical performances, or else the offspring of a subtile vanity and desire for intellectual sympathy. Let one persuade many, and he becomes confirmed and convinced, and cares for no better evidence. Men will not agree in the fashions of their dress, in manners, or "beliefs," till reduced to the naked facts of experience; and the precepts and methods of modern science, every day extended to new fields of inquiry, will, in these, I believe, do more to invigorate and correct the human understanding than all the essays of all the philosophers.

The old philosophy is ignored by science, not opposed by it, and must take its chance in the reconstruction of speculative thought without the aid of the traditions, the loyalties, and the patriotisms which now certify so much to so many. Why are we Protestants rather than Catholics, Unitarians rather than Orthodox, radicals rather than reactionists? Certainly, not for the kind of reason which makes us Newtonians.

Positivism, to be sure, so far as it pretends to be a philosophy at all, is more than the body of the sciences. It must be a system of the universal methods, hypotheses, and principles which are founded on them, and if not a universal science, in an absolute sense, yet must be coextensive with actual knowledge, and exhibit the consilience of the sciences.

But while positivism ignores religion in the narrower sense of the word—that is, the body thereof—it nevertheless, unlike the old atheism, does not reject the religious spirit. It is rather constrained—not for itself, but through the earnest, practical characters of many of its disciples—to yield some worthy object to religious devotion, which they think they find in the interests of humanity. But this is an affair of character, not of intelligence. If you define the end of philosophy to be the attainment of religious objects and truths, then positivism is no philosophy. The religion of positivism is no part of its philosophy, but is only a religion which consists with its rigid methods and restraints. Mr. Mill maintains that such a religion is not only possible, but has actually controlled the lives and formed the characters of men of this way of thinking.

I see that, after declining to enter into this discussion in your book, I have straightway been tempted to take it up in my letter; but my aim is only to show how such an essay as you desire would not properly come from one who is a positivist in spite of religion: it should rather come from someone who is religious in spite of his positivism. I could do better in the way of defending this philosophy from theological attacks than in adapting a religion to it.

I hope to hear from you soon, in spite of my ill-deserts, and to hear that you are prospering.

To Miss Jane Norton [4]

Cambridge, March 22, 1869.

I cannot believe that you designedly imposed on me, as a punishment, the difficult task (which would require much reflection) of giving clear and satisfactory reasons for my refusal of Mr. Abbot's proposition about the Essay on the Religious Aspects of Positivism; but I feel myself in the condition of the schoolboy who can only answer the demand to explain his misconduct by the summary but inexplicit reason "because"—by which he enounces, at least, his faith in the universality of causation, or in the doctrine of "the sufficient reason" without which nothing happens.

It might possibly be easier to write the essay than to say why not do it. Both would be difficult expositions, and to attempt the essay would, perhaps, be the directest means of demonstrating my incompetency—at least my present incompetency. . . . There may appear but a shade of difference between a general essay on the religious bearings of positivism and a defense of this philosophy, and its adherents, from the attacks and misrepresentations of theological opponents. But the difference is really material. I may be the swiftest racer on this course; yet to no purpose, since I lack rider and spur. If I were more of a Comtist than I am, that is, had a proselyting interest in the direct practical bearings of positivism, I should rush, I suppose, to a platform or into print before the great and discriminating public. As it is, I have much greater confidence in the indirect influence of the causes, which have made this philosophy prevail, to determine and exert its religious effects than I have in the discussion of themes which in the common estimation are more specifically religious.

Our side cannot now help being heard on its substantial merits, and has no need of pulpits. The effect on the characters

[4] [Houghton, bMs Am 1088.1, 106.]

and directions of men's faiths, which the possession of a large and extensive body of unquestionable and united truths is fitted to produce, is one which follows naturally, in whatever direction this body of knowledge has disciplined the philosophical dispositions to act within the legitimate limits of speculation. To take in enough of natural philosophy to make one feel sure that the weather is not ruled by any free moral agents, though it diminishes many other assurances (much supposed weather-wisdom) is yet a great step in advance. To take such steps in social science must have the effect to turn men's attention to new social interests, no longer directly dependent on the social powers of the prayerful, the hopeful, the angry, the willful, or the affectionate child, but on those of the foreseeing, contriving, intelligent man. Moral effort, though, as before, arising in these burnings of the heart, will then gain through its light a far-reaching influence, which its warmth does not possess.

On this aspect of the subject I might write to the verge of sentimentality; but this, I suppose, is not what Mr. Abbot wanted from my pen. What positivism has to say about the great religious doctrines of "supernatural causes" and "the future life" is the question of the theologically trained mind; and if positivism has nothing to say on these things how can it justify its pretension to be a philosophy and a competent guide of life. In this question of authority its not unskillful opponents strike at a vital point; but the blow can be parried and in return positivism can more pertinently demand of the so-called religious philosophies *their* authority for saying anything on these themes. That life would not be worth improving, moral effort vain, without some such grounds of action as religion presents; that any questions of them must be settled before life can have an intelligent interest for us, or show human nature to be superior to the brutal—to such replies the kind of return, which positivism is most naturally and charitably inclined to, is not polemical but hygienic. The formidable aspects of these themes, the associations of feelings which have grown up with them, are of the nature of diseases, infectious or transmitted, but not unavoidable at the outset (as our ignorance and the limits of our possible development are). They are traditional distortions of development, which the natural man even in attaining the most advanced moral growth need not undergo. This view of the matter (the doctrine of distorted development) is the positive counterpart of the orthodox doctrine of "original depravity." The cure should not be "heroic," since this method attacks the patient as well as the disease. Opening to his activity a mental and moral and even philosophical life, infinitely varied in objects which invite attention and incite to effort, and wide enough for a rational spirit of speculation (the pursuits of positive science and their various directions)—complete preoccupation is the true treatment. If this should be objected to as practically only a culture in "*mere* morality," it would be, as Mr. Emerson says, "as much as if one should say, 'Poor God with nobody to help him.' "

In my former correspondence with Mr. Abbot about the direct bearings of positivism on the subjects of religion I was conscious of adopting in a mild way the heroic treatment, attacking under indirect forms, not his opinions, but the still too superstitious spirit in which he seemed to me to hold them—in which he seemed to attribute still in his understanding the weight of valid evidence to the force of merely associated interests. To dissociate these interests, not to criticize his doctrines, was my only end in the debate; and I should not be willing to enter again into any such debate, except it be again with a person equally candid, unprejudiced, and intelligent—certainly not with the public. My regard for the social and political attitude of radicalism, as the extreme and yet the logically valid result of Protestantism, is very widely separated from my interest in the several philosophies, practical and speculative, which in the minds of the several radicals is so intimately (and to them so naturally) associated with this attitude. As a distinct body of religious thinkers, or other than as a few among liberals of many varieties, I have little sympathy with them, and not much respect for their intelligence. Perhaps you will think me even a little prejudiced; but between Dr. Peabody and Mrs. Howe it is hard to choose.[5]

I have so little space left to tell the news in (or even to make such a sharp turn and deep descent) that I am constrained to regard this as *the* essay in question (abortive and abbreviated though it be), instead of the letter I meant to write.

To Mr. Norton [6]

Cambridge, Aug. 10, 1870.

Utility does not oppose itself, as many intuitive or sentimental moralists suppose, to the proper jurisdiction of feeling—to devotion, or to the passionate love of the beautiful. Its philosophy does not contend for the sanction of utility as the sole and sufficing motive to conduct. It only proposes a standard as the proper test—a negative test it may be—of every motive. It does not propose to measure beforehand the positive elements of possible human excellences, the highest aims or the supremest delights. Its real enemy is a priori conviction, or prejudice asserting itself as its own justification, or sentiment born of strife and narrowness, and sanctioned only by custom and traditional religious authority. So far as a feeling is ultimate and an immediate source of human happiness or excellence, it is its own positive standard and sanction. Utility tests it only negatively in its consistency with other interests and feelings and with the maximum of all in all sentient beings, measured both by intensity and rank (not moral rank, for this is a resultant, an acquired or conferred dignity). The inductions and criticisms by which this test is applied may be long and difficult and may not be possible for an individual observer of social conditions

5 [Andrew Preston Peabody (1811-1893), a conservative religious thinker, was appointed Plummer Professor of Christian Morals at Harvard in 1862. Julia Ward Howe (1819-1910) was a liberal religious thinker and an enthusiastic reformer.]

6 [Houghton, bMs Am 1088, 8291.]

(like the inductions of astronomy or other physical sciences), but as the result of many centuries of observation they are embodied in the best or wisest moral codes or exemplars, which come to us sanctioned by many associations, not in themselves rightly authoritative, but often more influential (and usefully so) than their rational grounds could be, except with the most refined and enlightened.

There is an antithesis between utility and beauty, between the useful and the beautiful, which is often mistaken for an antagonism. A useful thing is a means simply, and not an end in itself. A beautiful thing belongs to the class of ends in themselves, or absolute ends, to which also belongs every ultimate source of pleasure of whatever rank or intensity. The beautiful thing agrees with the class to which it belongs in having no ulterior end, or only an incidental one (like Mr. Darwin's uses of color in birds and flowers), but it differs from its class generally in having a high rank, an intrinsic dignity, or preferability in kind, which depends on its mental relationships and affinities. But whether the pursuit of the beautiful be right or wrong is not determined by its rank as a pleasure, although this rank, depending on its broad relationships, would be likely enough to insure that consistency with the maximum of excellence, or happiness, or pleasure, or well-being, or by whatever name we call the true ultimate standard of moral excellence. Now so far is the pursuit of the useful from being inconsistent with the pursuit of the beautiful, that it really presupposes such ultimate ends as the grounds of its utility. But it is not the beautiful alone or even pre-eminently, but the whole class of ends in themselves—all our pleasures and those of all sentient beings—that constitute the grounds of utility. It is a mistake, however, which all, or almost all, the opponents of the utilitarian philosophy make, as well as many of its advocates, to suppose that the measure of a pleasure in this philosophy is simply its intensity as a feeling and not also its rank or preferability in kind, or a certain dignity it has in the spiritual hierarchy independent of and antecedent to its proper moral rank. This moral rank is a derived dignity, and is determined by preferability or weight with the will on the whole and as compared with the *sum* of the pleasures or ends that are sacrificed for it, both in ourselves and others. But in this estimate the intrinsic value of a pleasure, independent of its intensity and depending on its extent in our natures and in our lives, should be taken into account. Thus the intuitive moralist is correct in affirming intrinsic differences of dignity in ends, at least as motives in the developed will, or in any but the most elementary of mental natures; but he errs again in supposing that these are the same as moral differences or original distinctions of right and wrong. They are unquestionably the grounds which, along with the intensities of feelings as pleasures or pains, determine the moral rank of actions or rules of conduct.

To allow these original differences of rank in ends may seem to be granting to the intuitive moralist all that he demands, and leaving nothing distinctive in the utilitarian philosophy. But this is far from being the case either theoretically or practically. In theory this philosophy has still to insist distinctively that no rule or principle of conduct, except its own fundamental maxim of the greatest universal benevolence and disinterestedness, can be received on the authority of any sense or sentiment or properly intuitive power, or be ultimately and authoritatively determined to be right, except by the longest acquaintance with the conditions of well-being and the general consequences or effects on well-being of acting on the rule. Some of the most fundamental and important rules of morality, chiefly negative in form, are, it is true, quite simple corollaries from obvious conditions of well-being and the fundamental axiom of the greatest good; and it is also true practically that more influential sanctions than utility are necessary to enforce its injunctions, and are therefore sanctioned by it. Moreover what is called the conscience, or strong and controlling aversions to certain classes of actions and admirations or approvals of other classes, should be respected and carefully fostered, even though in some matters it leads wrong; since a faulty conscience is more useful or less harmful on the whole than unprincipled conduct even in the best disposed natures. But practically also the utilitarian philosophy has a distinctive lesson to teach, or rather many lessons—a whole world of abuses to correct, which subsist by the very same sanctions or the same kind of sanctions that the intuitive morality adopts as the basis of right and wrong. Such are the self-sanctioned prejudices, time-sanctioned iniquities, religious absurdities, all of which can claim the same grounds of justification as those on which the intuitive morality would base the ten commandments, namely, that most people, or at least somebody, *feels* them to be right. That somebody, say the pope, should be infallible in his feelings is a necessary cornerstone of this philosophy, and most of the unorthodox or radical advocates of it claim this infallibility for themselves; but it follows from their principles that in cases of dispute some pope, whether the Roman pontiff or not, some holiest man, must be the final arbiter.

The aims and lessons of the utilitarian philosophy are not, however, in any way opposed to, but are rather in alliance with, all that is noble and beautiful and delightful in the possibilities of human nature. It is only incidentally or perhaps by a mistake of its true scope and interests that it turns attention away from aesthetic pursuits to the broader but perhaps on the whole not worthier interests of science or industry or politics.

I do not think that you at all overestimate the spiritual rank of aesthetic pleasures. They are intimately associated with the fundamental quality of moral nobility; they consist with generosity and sympathy, and are inconsistent with monopoly, thus differing from merely sensual pleasures, though like these they are ends in themselves. Again they are refined pleasures. All that is disagreeable or loathsome is removed; and the special end of the Fine Arts is this refinement or abstraction of the beautiful. Moreover they are pleasures of the higher senses and have extensive intellectual affinities. This is Mr. Bain's [7] analysis, which, whether complete or not, is the best I have seen. Aesthetic pleasures doubtless belong, as you say, to the most sensi-

[7] [Alexander Bain (1818-1903), Scottish philosopher and educationist. Cf. *The Senses and the Intellect* (1855, revised ed. in 1894) and *The Emotions and the Will* (1859).]

tive, susceptible, and passionate natures, and they were doubtless more pursued, but I think for a different reason and not from temperament, by the men of the thirteenth century than by those of the nineteenth. There is nothing in the aims of our times inconsistent with them except, perhaps, the catholicity and variety of modern interests, and a consequent want of concentration and general sympathy and of public patronage of them. Instead of whole communities devoting their surplus wealth to them, and reinforcing them with the powerful sentiments of patriotism and religion, we have now, and probably can have, only schools or at best colonies of artists, who must inevitably seem narrow in their aims compared to the men with whom Art meant not only beauty but the highest honors, and public spirit, and religion. A great general may be entirely absorbed in the problems of the art of war, but his enthusiasm for his pursuit cannot be said to be independent of the patriotic ardor of his soldiers. And so though no doubt as you say the best Gothic artists were distinctly and consciously moved not through devout passion but through plain aesthetic joy, yet the intensity and quality of their feeling must have depended on an appreciation of their work which sprung from other than aesthetic motives, from national or race pride, from patriotism or religious devotion. Indeed as you go on to say the happiness of the Gothic artists was "in the successful solution of problems they had to solve. It was the delight of beauty *joined with* the excitement of genuine scientific achievements"; but this adjunct is not an aesthetic motive, though it be the last infirmity of noble minds.

To Miss Grace Norton [8]

July 29, 1874.

I have just tried my butterfly nature in search of summer sweets. I spent Friday night at Blue Hill with the Putnams. On Saturday I flitted to Portsmouth, going in the evening on a

[8] [Houghton, bMs Am 1088.1, 307.]

picnic, up with the tide, on the banks of the Piscataqua, and floating, after tea, down the tide in the moonlight very romantically. On Sunday Mr. Emery and I walked or crawled to York, visited our friends, the Brookses, of Cambridge, absorbed the beauties of the place by sunset, and returned by moonlight—a round trip afoot of more than twenty miles. Mr. Emery is an excellent traveling companion, devoted mainly to the business afoot. . . . We only settled on the walk one important question, which Clifford Watson at the picnic had propounded from his experience in boating. We, or at least I, concluded that the question was to be decided by moral not mechanical causes, and I generalized that in the moral world difficulty increases success instead of diminishing it, as in mechanical efforts, and that the problems of boating were threefold, or depended on three classes of *momenta*—the purely mechanical, the physiological, and the moral, the several advantages of which have in practice to be duly adjusted; a very *owl-wise* settlement of the practical question!

On Monday I had no disposition to walk but took wing again and alighted on the way back at Magnolia, where I found my young friend, Meggie Lesley, and several other friends. Mrs. Lesley was gone away for a visit of a few days. Yesterday brought me back here to the old grub-chamber, a still living, full-grown, full-blown, and perhaps full-flown *imago;* whether thus ephemeral, or whether I may go farther, is as yet undeveloped in my moral consciousness. Invitations to Mount Desert, to Northampton, to Florida Mountain, and neither last nor least, to Ashfield, are prophetic of a longer winged life. . . .

I do not feel so confident about your problem, "Why do *we* exist?" Not that I believe there is any essential mystery in the nature of things other than what an idle question-asking habit gratuitously imports into them for the sake of wonder—a rather dry and superfluous fodder for that divine sentiment! All the ends of life are, I am persuaded, within the sphere of life and are in the last analysis, or highest generalization, to be found in the preservation, continuance, and increase of life itself, in all its quantities of rank, intensity, and number, which exists—"for what" do you ask? Why, for nothing, to be sure! Quite gratuitously. Does anyone seriously expect to be answered in any other terms than those in which the question could be rationally framed? Are any ends suggested out of the sphere of life itself? If not, this is an aimless curiosity. Interrogation is reduced by it to the point which one may answer thus—?! . . .

The *social* value of questions is indeed a matter we might overlook in a too serious purpose to find their answers. The social value of the weather is nothing to theirs, and insoluble questions have a permanent value of this sort. Religions are founded on them.

Still in the interest of sober inquisitiveness, it might be worth while to root out some of these questions for the sake of others more genuine. Let the questions of the uses of life then be put in this shape: To what ascertainable form or phase of life is this or that other form or phase of life valuable or serviceable? If we fail in this direction we need not be quite nonplussed, for no form of movement in life is without a value in itself. It is not pleasures alone that would go on if they were permitted. Pains and griefs hug themselves sometimes and think they have the same right to last; and the nobler ones even win the will over to their conservation. I am more than half persuaded that most, if not all, of the puzzles of metaphysics may be reduced to unconscious puns or unseen ambiguities in terms. Now "life" means in common discourse two things very different, but easily confounded. We sometimes mean by "life" what is comprised in the plans, purposes, inquisitions, and aspirations that make ambition and the zests of curiosity and anticipation so large a part of the conscious life of youth. Well, if for any cause (an indigestion, for example), the strength and zest that went in search of these goods of life happen to fail, we say we have tried life and exhausted its resources! It has no more value for us. We are ready to die! If we meditate suicide, it is not our duty to others nor the rights others may have in our lives that should restrain us. We are more irrational than to merely forget the claims of conscience. We suffer from a mental indigestion. We have not solved the ambiguities of words.

The *life* we would attack is not the culprit. The kind of dying which a wise moralist would enjoin is the death of the unsatisfied anticipations, curiosities, ambitions, which, fixed as habits, still linger and distress the soul, since the strength and zest have failed which could give them further fruition. But these forms of life die without sacrificing one's usefulness or duties to others or without cutting off a host of resources which come in old age to make "life" quite tolerable. "As to exhausting life objectively," the wise moralist would add, "that is sheer illusion, even if you happen to be an Alexander. Gain back the nerve, the strength, the zest, and you have gained back the world with its inexhaustible resources." But the true philosophical way is to look on life as it is, as somewhat broader than the fading pictures, plans, and purposes which you have mistaken for it, and as consisting in more than that set of inveterate habits which you call yourself. The death you should desire is the death of those desires which, like all unsupported or no longer satisfied impulses of habit or instinct, have become pains. Work in other channels and thus immolate yourself, and you will not find an end of life desirable. Life in this wider sense is neither good nor evil, but the theater of possible goods and evils. There is no choice between it and death, not because their claims are equal but because real unillusioned choice lies wholly within the sphere of life. The will is constrained between this and that form of life and is never impelled to real unconsciousness. We desire sleep, it is true, but rationally in only two ways, neither of which is unconsciousness, namely, first, the falling asleep as an immediate end or pleasure in itself, and, secondly, sound sleep as a means to the anticipated end of a refreshed and invigorated waking. All the rest is beyond our choice, a matter of fate and automatic change, or else of frenzied action under the influence of illusion—the illusion that death resembles sleep in anything for which sleep can be desired. There is never any real choice between a state of consciousness, however painful, and unconsciousness—no real movement of the will that way—though there is an illusory superficial resemblance to unconsciousness in vague anticipations of more pleasurable conditions than those we seek to escape.

The penalty, I suppose, for disobeying these wise directions is to be judged foolish. I agree with this wise councilor that life in general exists for nothing. The impossibility of really wishing for annihilation, or for real unconsciousness, is however no evidence to me, as it is to the mystics, that there is no such thing, or that the fates, of which my choice is no part, have not this condition in store into which to turn me, as automatic changes in life put me into a soundness of sleep in itself undesired, however pleasant the way to it or the refreshment of waking from it may be.

To limit the question of rational ends to the sphere of life is to bring a host of questions to light touching the dependence of one form of life on another, which to the moralist as well as the naturalist promise more than the gratification of a prurient wonder at insoluble mysteries, and are more than topics of social incitement. . . .

What a narrow, selfish, childish, and egotistical philosophy is that of the poets and sentimentalists who look on life as a playground which they think their Maker has laid out for their delectation: whereas it is for keeping their race a-going (or was), whatever the use of that may be. There is one among that sort of philosophers who has caught a glimpse of this great natural truth in what his disciples call "Newman's principle"—an important half-truth. "You will not be happy," he says, "unless you are virtuous; but you will not be virtuous, if you seek for happiness." No wise utilitarian would be disposed to question this as a psychological fact, but none would accept the paradox as an ultimate theoretical principle of morals. And there are not wanting illustrative parallels to it in the natural science of life. Nature puts the most important functions of life in charge of automatic and instinctive agents which have their own most vigilant and effective motives. These are sometimes so independent of the will that even a favoring interference of this general governor disconcerts the special agent and frustrates the common purpose. Thus we sneeze much more vigorously against our wills than with their aid; which, if too eager to promote the action, may actually suspend it or prevent it altogether. The same is true of an acquired nature or habit. If we, or our reasons, distrust any one of our acquired dexterities and attempt by attention to help it out, we are apt to put it quite out of kilter or to paralyze its proper efficiency. Every habit (and virtue, as Aristotle taught, is a habit) is its own motive, its own "excuse for being"—or one of its excuses. The pains of disconcerted or frustrated habits and the inherent pleasure there is in following them are motives which nature has put into our wills without generally caring to inform us why, and she sometimes decrees indeed that her reasons shall not be ours. So that practically we find ourselves acting the more reasonably and more for the real ends of nature in proportion as these are not our immediate motives, but give place to more completely devoted, single-purposed, and therefore effective powers, or to instincts and habits; which we should nevertheless as reasonable beings subject theoretically, or in our philosophy of life and duty, to the test of the good they subserve in the economy of life.

Utilitarianism needs to be supplemented, in order to meet misunderstandings, by a Philosophy of Habit, and to lay down among its practical principles that, since motives are effective not in proportion to their usefulness or reasonableness but rather to their singleness or instinctiveness, therefore it is reasonable to foster and to rely practically on the force of proper habits and just natural inclinations. In the serene and unopposed play of these—and especially in their concord or harmonious play—there is a source of happiness to the agent which the sentimental moralist mistakes for the real, or natural, end of virtue but which belongs to it only as a habit, or as a body of mutually supporting or concordant habits; and is quite distinct from the happiness or well-being to which as virtuous or reasonable habits and inclinations they are or should be adapted. Dignity is a weight with the will, or an effective source of happiness, which these powers of habit and instinct gain from their mutual support or harmonious action and from their persistent influence and which would be the natural result of accordance with the harmonious real ends of life. It is to questioned and artificial rules of life and to the morals of legislation rather than to the instincts of the individual conscience that the utilitarian test is of greatest practical importance. Nature has not waited for human reason to discover or to test all the instincts and disciplines best adapted for keeping the surviving races of men in the most flourishing condition, just as she did not wait for physiological science to disclose the uses of color, but secured them in her economy by making them the delight and one, apparently, of the most important ends of vision, though really one, as we have seen, of its most important means.

To Miss Grace Norton [9]

Aug. 12, 1874.

You say that while you do not believe the noblest end of life to be "serviceableness," in the ordinary meaning of the word—"whatever it may be as an aim" (proximate end?); yet you still less believe that in the last analysis we should find the ends of life in the preservation, continuance, and increase of life itself. I agree entirely with you about "serviceableness" as an end, that is, serviceableness as such, for this would be a foolish confusion of the essence of means with ends; though, as one of "a Christian's" delights and blissful habits or virtues, it doubtless makes part of the noble "perfectness" of individual human existence. This "perfectness" which you contrast with the preservation, etc., of life I meant to include in what, as I recollect, I added as the *quantity in worth, dignity, or rank* in the increase of life, its quantity in intensity and number being other parts of it as a final cause. What do we really mean, understandingly (not emotionally), by the words "perfectness," "dignity," "absolute worth" ? The mystic who finds God in the inward perfectness he dreams of in himself thinks it the end of

[9] [Houghton, bMs Am 1088.1, 308.]

the universe, whereas I think its dignity is limited to that spiritual mechanism of the human flower which is most purely and concentratedly serviceable to that *whole* life of mankind which reproduces and embodies it. Dignity, as I think I defined it in another connection, is a weight with the will, or a power as a motive, which depends on the mutual support that what we therefore call our virtues get from one another, and from all the motives of life in their most complete harmony and consistency. Mysticism is so stupid and spiritually self-engrossed that the better self, which it ought to contemplate as a particular representative of the endless solidarity of human life, is thought of by it as the individual mystic's immortal part. Mysticism is so blindly self-engrossed that it cannot understand utilitarianism but supposes this doctrine to mean a service of the higher or the virtuous inclinations of our nature to the lower, or merely to the gross well-being of human life. Utilitarianism does not mean this, though this is a *part* of its meaning. The lower *so far as* they are the conditions of the higher; the appetites *so far as* they are also essential to the preservation, continuance, and increase of life; the passions *so far as* their singleness or instinctiveness is serviceable to the whole—are, in a stricter sense, ends or final causes even [more] than is that perfectness of virtue which is its own reward. So far as the happiness of virtue depends on its being a fixed habit, as it does in the egotistic regard of the Pharisee, so far it has no more worth, dignity, or perfectness than any instinct or any other habit in itself. But so far as any habit, on the other hand, is not opposed by equally strong and persistent motives but is in wide and strong alliance with others which, with it, are therefore named "reasonable" or "virtuous," it is an integrant part of a system of dispositions which, as superintending, so far as it goes, the whole of the conditions of human life, and leading to the conservation of the whole, itself included, is what we call *conscience*, and is preeminently a final cause in human nature.

Now utilitarians have consciences as well as the sentimentalists. Their philosophy concerns itself with the conscience of conscience, with its truest harmony, or with its reasonableness, with the accordance of everything in it with the least doubtful of its behests. "Nature," says Cicero, "has inclined us to love of mankind; and this is the foundation of laws" (*fundamentum juris*). This is both the rational and the disciplinary foundation, the ground and the efficacy of laws, since fear becomes a moral power only by its sanction; and even those laws which we may be said to observe instinctively, or as ends from the start and in themselves, are instinctively associated with the love of mankind, with the wish for the greatest good of the greatest number. On this wish hang all the law and the prophets.

The *reliance* of utilitarians on their philosophy, which, in consideration of their acknowledgment of the essential value of instincts and habits, though not of the ultimate authority of these, gives you so much surprise—this reliance is not different from what the disciples of any other creed have on a philosophy that professes to be the *guide* of life. It is not a reliance on the ability of the individual reason to review in the light of fundamental principles the whole range of possible moral actions. It is not even a reliance on the whole *reflective* experience of mankind as transmitted in customs and traditions. The reliance of experiential philosophers in general is not on the ability of each investigator to verify by experiment and observation what he nevertheless has good reason to accept as true laws of nature and as really verifiable, nor is it on the completeness of what has been already ascertained experimentally. It is a reliance on *its method*, whenever or wherever any method is needed. But the reasonableness of many enjoined customs and rules of life is of a negative sort—the nonexistence of anything truly obligatory that is really seen to be opposed to them. This proves their harmlessness at least so far as we can see, and wherever they seem to have a foundation in instinct (like the horror of suicide or murder) there is a positive presumption that they are somewhat more than merely harmless injunctions. Yet in this they have to the utilitarian nothing more than a presumption of obligation, for inherited instincts are not always right or useful to present conditions of a progressive form of life. They may have made the whole transit from what *ought* to what *ought not* to be obeyed, though still remaining instincts in our nature, like fear and rage; or even though in the individual will they may have the pervasiveness and the permanent sway of a rational principle. The large part which the authority of teachers and force-sanctioned laws have in our moral life affords indeed a presumption against the trustworthiness of instincts in general, and when a seemingly instinctive inclination receives sanction in customs and early discipline it is often difficult to distinguish how much training has added to nature: for the consciences of savages differ from ours in both respects, and more discipline is needed for some of our youths than for others.

What utilitarianism *distrusts*, therefore, is the authority of mere strength or earnestness of moral feelings or injunctions when set up as a reason for conduct. But this does not mean an habitual distrust in the utilitarian of his own conscientious feelings, nor a doubt of them leading to the abrogation of their actual authority or weight with his will. Earnestness is a proof of conscientiousness, not of the rightness of a conscience, or is the measure of efficacy rather than of rectitude, and is often much greater in respect to mere superstitions and rules of etiquette than to the most certain of moral principles. For earnestness is oftener the result of that love for mankind which takes the form of reverence for teachers or of following the supposed divine in human examples than of that love for mankind which should (but, unfortunately, not always does) guide the reason of the leader and teacher.

This distrust becomes a positive rejection on the part of this philosophy of any authority in the earnestness of a feeling when this is brought into the judgment, or rational trial, of a rule of conduct in any real dispute concerning it. In any real dispute about the wisdom or rectitude of a moral rule (not about the motives of a moral agent), utilitarianism takes the reins of judgment into its own hands, then actually asserting what is always its prerogative, the supremacy of its tests over all authorities—tests supreme, so far as they are seen to go, even over the universal instincts of men; since only so far as these can be seen, or else presumed to be allied with the love and service of mankind, can they be justified; and utilitarianism sits in permanent judgment over all law-*making*, over all devices of expediency, whether these be deductions from laws or exceptions to the existing and acknowledged rules of duty. Its reliance on the forces of habit and instinct is not for rational guidance but for practical efficacy, yet these are so important to its aims that they are not safely to be disregarded or unnecessarily opposed or weakened by substituting for them habitually the calculations of expediency. The mystic who mistakes for the final causes of the universe that better part in himself which, as the representative of all human interests, is a final cause of the universe of human life, dreams in his conceit that he is God, and that stars and flowers as well as statues exist for him and for his equals in immortality. He lays down his life, if at all, for the furthering of his own inward bliss (as he dreams) or for heaven instead of for the furtherance of nature's care in life for the whole, in which sooner or later he must disappear. . . .

III

THEORY OF KNOWLEDGE AND METAPHYSICS

[THE NATURE OF A PRIORI KNOWLEDGE]

To Mr. Abbot [1]

Cambridge, Oct. 28, 1867.

I was very glad to hear again so soon from you on the subjects of our debate, and to know that you still retain so fresh an interest in them in spite of your recent losses and perplexities.[2]

Your letter interests me very much. It is so full of suggestive points, and affords so much light to me on the real grounds of our differences, that I hardly feel able in the limited space of a letter to say all I wish to on its various topics. The most profitable discussion is, after all, a study of other minds—seeing how others see, rather than the dissection of mere propositions. The restatement of fundamental doctrines in new connections affords a parallax of their philosophical standpoints (unless these be buried in the infinite depths), which adds much to our knowledge of one another's thought.

Concerning the foundation of experientialism, I agree with you "that experience includes more than a heterogeneous mass

1 [*Letters,* pp. 123-129.]

2 [Mr. Abbot was at this time a Unitarian clergyman at Dover, New Hampshire. The allusion is to difficulties which arose out of a growing divergence between the opinions held by him and those commonly held by his denomination. These controversies culminated in litigation of a very interesting character, of which an account may be found in the case of Hale v. Everett, 53 *New Hampshire Reports* p. 1.—Thayer's note.]

of particular sensuous impressions, and cannot be explained by a mere 'law of association' among such impressions." Our cognitions are indeed more than the mere chronicles of a sensuous history. There are orders and forms in them which do not come directly from the transient details of sense perceptions. Indeed, without the constant reaction of the mind through memory upon the presentations of the senses, there could arise nothing worth the name of knowledge. If our memories were only retentive and not also co-operative with the senses, only associations of the very lowest order could be formed. We should not each know the same world, but only each his own world. It is only by the accumulation, the prepetual sifting, and the thoroughgoing comparison of impressions, associating, dissociating, and reassociating them according to laws of understanding, that the order of true cognition is finally brought out of the chaos of sensuous impressions. This order, once established to any degree, exercises a constant control over the senses and governs our attention in perception. This ferment of the mind, giving rise to an intellectual order, establishes the strongest associations among its elements, and some associations which are insoluble.

This process is not determined solely by the laws of association among the elements of the primitive impressions. There is always an a priori or mnemonic element involved. Associations, either original to the mind or early established, control the formation of new ones. Of the manifold of a presentation, only parts are retained in the mind and remain adherent to one another; and this selection is determined a priori, by the orders of impressions already experienced, or else by an order inherent in the very nature of the intellect.

The "a priori theory" holds that this final order of cognition belongs to a pre-existent *intellectus ipse,* and is, in some respects at least, independent of the primitive orders of sense associations. It holds that the final products of understanding contain elements not contained in the primitive impressions and educible by the permutations of them in reflection. It holds, in other words, that the higher faculties of knowledge are like the organs of sense, already existent and equipped for action prior to the occasions and independently of the matter of knowledge; that thinking is a process performed on the impressions of sense by powers which are not in any way determined by the matter of thoughts, and which consequently add to the result elements not contained in the sense impressions.

If I understand the form in which you hold to this doctrine, it is that the elements added by understanding are objective ones, not forms of understanding but facts of experience which the understanding intuits in sense impressions. As the material forces of light, heat, sound, pressure, and chemical change could not of themselves, without the organs of sense, produce the sense impressions, so neither can these pass on of their own inherent powers into abstract thought, but must come into the form of thought through a pre-existent organ of thought, acting by laws peculiar to itself. The *relations* of sensible objects—the *twoness* of two hats, the *superposition* of the book *on* the shelf, and the like matters of thought—are not, according to you, intuited by sense, any more than the color of a sonorous body is intuited by hearing or the tone of a colored body by sight. If we could not be conscious of the two hats without being conscious that they are *two*, or conscious of the book and the shelf without being conscious that the book is *on* the shelf, this would only prove that the understanding acts simultaneously with the sense, and that only the vaguest sense impressions can be cognized without an action of the understanding upon them, to discover their relations.

To this I fully agree. In fact, I would go further and maintain that there is no cognition by the senses in contradistinction from the mental powers generally. Instead of allowing two orders of independent cognitions, those of the senses and those of the intellect, I would maintain that all cognitions alike involve understanding in some degree, or some relation of the new impression to the previous content of the mind. An impression is cognized only when brought into consciousness, that is, into relations with what we have previously thought or felt or desired.

Nevertheless, I regard as valid the distinction of intuitive and abstract cognitions. The first we have without any consciousness of its cause, that is, without any other mental facts preceding and generating it in a recognizable general process of which we may be reflectively conscious. Abstract cognitions we have as consequent upon others, and may attend to the process of their generation. In both, there is a sensuous basis, though not one separately cognizable. I can realize in thought a relation, like superposition, only by imagining things in this relation—that is, by having subjectively determined sense impressions of some things superposed on other things; and I arrive at the abstract notion of superposition by attending to compound objects which resemble each other in this respect, like my hat on my head, the book on the shelf, the inkstand on the table, etc. I maintain that relations which can by abstraction be thought as in objects must exist in objects as intuited, and also that the intuition must be more or less understood—brought under classes or associated with previous experience—in order to be properly cognized at all.

You would regard the *color* and the *shape* of an object as intuited by two distinctly different modes of mental action. The sense of sight cognizes the color, the understanding the shape; for the shape can only be cognized by comparison with abstract forms, which "brings the object into relation" with other objects. But I maintain that the color of the object is cognized in precisely the same way, as being like or unlike the color of other objects. The color announces itself—is presented to consciousness—by rousing all the colors of memory which similitude or contrast can by association connect with it. This is a process of which we are distinctly conscious only in its effect, as when we name the color. Without some movement toward this reasoning, there is no attention to the color, no cognition, no effective intuition. When this movement is also cognized as a process of thought, the cognition ceases to be intuitive—is the result of conscious understanding—but is none the less a movement of impressions, either objectively or subjectively determined, which are as sensuous as color. It is true, as you say, that "in the book singly, or in the shelf singly, there is no relation of superposition"; but the fact that you can attend to them singly, abstracting the relation, does not prove that, after being presented, they need to be "brought into relation" by an act of understanding. It is by an abstractive act, indeed, that you attend to them singly and out of the relation which is as much in the sensuous intuition of them as their colors or shapes. It is a favorite formula with me that there are two kinds of memory or reminiscence—the memory of representation and the memory of judgment. In the first, we recognize singular facts of experience individually; in the second, in their generalized results. In the first, through the pictures of imagination; in the second, by the language of abstract thought. Every item of experience adds to the cogency of a common-sense judgment, though not distinctly recognized or consciously added to the weight of evidence. But, if it is recognized as a ground of evidence, it must be as an instance of a rule, or as a fact similar to other facts. For what is it in the intuition which is cognizable, unless it be its likeness or unlikeness to other intuitions? The book on the shelf, the hat on the head, the inkstand on the table, are similar compound or plural objects in respect to the relation of superposition. This similitude is not apprehended by the senses independently of mental operations; but neither is the color nor the weight nor the texture of these objects apprehended by the senses independently of memory, imagination, and abstraction.

What you call intellectual intuition I should regard as belonging to all cognitions alike. Indeed, the distinction between the intuitive and the nonintuitive knowledges is rather a logical than a psychological one. Cognitions which cannot be analyzed by introspection are called intuitions. These are the data, the axioms, the premises of logical processes; and the conclusions of such processes, being distinctly exhibited as consequent on other cognitions, are nonintuitive, derivative knowledges. But no amount of introspection can analyze a cognition down to the bare, unrelated data of the senses, strictly speaking; for this would be to dissolve all the links which bind the sensuous impression to consciousness, and to extrude it from the mind altogether.

But we may hypothetically descend to such a basis of knowledge. In accordance with physiological science, we may suppose, with Mill and Bain, that the higher mental faculties are formed by experience, that consciousness is a growth out of such primitive elements, a growth governed by laws of association, at first wholly chronological or by the association of contiguity, and afterwards more and more dependent, through memory, on associations of likeness and unlikeness. Though this theory has not yet shown itself competent to explain all mental phenomena satisfactorily, it has not been shown to be incompetent to this end, and seems to me in all respects a legitimate hypothesis. . . .

[THE STRUCTURE OF SELF-CONSCIOUSNESS]

The Evolution of Self-Consciousness[1]

The terms "science" and "scientific" have come, in modern times, to have so wide a range of application and so vague a meaning that (like many other terms, not only in common speech, but also in philosophy and in various branches of learning, like the law, which have come down to us through varying usages) they would oppose great difficulties to any attempts at defining them by *genus* and difference, or otherwise than by enumerating the branches of knowledge and the facts, or relations of the facts, to which usage has affixed them as names. Precision in proper definition being then impossible, it is yet possible to give to these terms so general a meaning as to cover all the knowledge to which they are usually applied, and still to exclude much besides. As the terms thus defined coincide with what I propose to show as the character of the knowledge

[1] [*North American Review,* CXVI (1873), 251-273.]

peculiar to men, or which distinguishes men's minds from those of other animals, I will begin with this definition. In science and in scientific facts there is implied a conscious purpose of including particular facts under general facts, and the less general under the more general ones. Science, in the modern use of the term, consists, essentially, of a knowledge of things and events either as effects of general causes, or as instances of general classes, rules, or laws; or even as isolated facts of which the class, law, rule, or cause is sought. The conscious purpose of arriving at general facts and at an adequate statement of them in language, or of bringing particular facts under explicit general ones, determines for any knowledge a scientific character.

Many of our knowledges and judgments from experience in practical matters are not so reduced, or sought to be reduced, to explicit principles, or have not a theoretical form, since the major premises, or general principles, of our judgments are not consciously generalized by us in forms of speech. Even matters not strictly practical, or which would be merely theoretical in their bearing on conduct, if reduced to a scientific form, like many of the judgments of common sense, for example, are not consciously referred by us to explicit principles, though derived, like science, from experience, and even from special kinds of experience, like that of a man of business or that of a professional adept. We are often led by being conscious of a sign of anything to believe in the existence of the thing itself, either past, present, or prospective, without having any distinct and general apprehension of the connection of the sign and thing, or any recognition of the sign under the general character of a sign. Not only are the judgments of common sense in men, both the inherited and acquired ones, devoid of heads or major premises (such as "All men are mortal") in deductive inference, and devoid also of distinctly remembered details of experience in the inferences of induction, but it is highly probable that this is all but exclusively the character of the knowledges and judgments of the lower animals. Language, strictly so called, which some of these animals also have, or signs *purposely used* for communication, is not only required for scientific knowledge, but a second step of generalization is needed, and is made through reflection by which this use of a sign is itself an object of attention, and the sign is recognized in its general relations to what it signifies, and to what it has signified in the past and will signify in the future. It is highly improbable that such a knowledge of knowledge, or such a *re*cognition, belongs in any considerable, or effective, degree to even the most intelligent of the lower animals, or even to the lowest of the human race. This is what is properly meant by being "rational" or being a "rational animal." It is what I have preferred to call "scientific" knowledge; since the growing vagueness and breadth of application common to all ill-comprehended words (like "Positivism" in recent times) have given to "scientific" the meaning probably attached at first to "rational." This knowledge comes from reflecting on what we know in the common-sense, or semi-instinctive form, or making what we know a field of renewed research, observation, and analysis in the generalization of major premises. The line of distinction between such results of reflection, or between scientific knowledge and the common-sense form of knowledge, is not simply the dividing line between the minds of men and those of other animals; but is that which divides the knowledge produced by outward attention from that which is further produced by reflective attention. The former, throughout a considerable range of the higher intelligent animals, involves veritable judgments of a complex sort. It involves combinations of minor premises leading to conclusions through implicit major premises in the enthymematic reasonings, commonly employed in inferences from signs and likelihoods, as in prognostications of the weather, or in orientations with many animals. This knowledge belongs both to men and to the animals next to men in intelligence, though in unequal degrees.

So far as logicians are correct in regarding an enthymeme as a reasoning, independently of its statement in words, or in regarding as a rational process the passing from such a sign as the human character of Socrates to the inference that he will die, through the data of experience concerning the mortality of other men—data which are neither distinctly remembered in detail nor generalized explicitly in the formula "all men are mortal," but are effective only in making mortality a more or less clearly understood part of the human character, that is, making it one of the attributes *suggested* by the name "man" yet not separated from the essential attributes by the contrasts of subject and attributes in real predication—so far, I say, as this can be regarded as a reasoning or a rational process, so far observation shows that the more intelligent dumb animals reason or are rational. But this involves great vagueness or want of that precision in the use of signs which the antitheses of essential and accidental attributes and that of proper predication secure. There is little or no evidence to show that the animals which learn, to some extent, to comprehend human speech have an analytical comprehension of real general propositions, or of propositions in which both subject and predicate are general terms and differ in meaning. A merely verbal general proposition, declaring only the equivalence of two general names, might be comprehended by such minds, if it could be made of sufficient interest to attract their attention. But this is extremely doubtful, and it would not be as a *proposition*, with its contrasts of essential and added elements of conception, that this would be comprehended. It would be, in effect, only repeating in succession two general names of the same class of objects. Such minds could, doubtless, comprehend a single class of objects, or an indefinite number of resembling things by several names; that is, several signs of such a class would recall it to their thoughts, or revive a representative image of it; and they would thus be aware of the equivalence of these signs; but they would not attach precision of meaning and different degrees of generality to them, or regard one name as the name or sign of another name; as when we define a triangle to be a rectilinear figure and a figure of three sides.

Only one degree of generality is, however, essential to inference from signs or in enthymematic reasoning. Moreover, language in its relations to thought does not consist exclusively of spoken or written or imagined words but of signs in general and, essentially, of internal images or successions of images, which are the representative imaginations of objects and their relations—imaginations which severally stand for each and all of the particular objects or relations of a *kind*. Such are the visual imaginations called up by spoken or written concrete general names of visible objects, as "dog" or "tree"; which are vague and feeble as images, but effective as notative, directive, or guiding elements in thought. These are the internal signs of things and events, and are instruments of thought in judgment and reasoning, not only with dumb animals but also with men, in whom they are supplemented, rather than supplanted, by names. But being of feeble intensity, and little under the influence of distinct attention or control of the will, compared to actual perceptions and to the voluntary movements of utterance and gesture, their nature has been but dimly understood even by metaphysicians, who are still divided into two schools in logic—the conceptualists and the nominalists. The "concepts" of the former are really composed of these vague and feeble notative images, or groups of images, to which clearness and distinctness of attention are given by their associations with outward (usually vocal) signs. Hence a second degree of observation and generalization upon these images, as objects in reflective thought, cannot be readily realized independently of what would be the results of such observations, namely, their associations with outward signs. They are probably so feeble, even in the most intelligent dumb animal, that they cannot be associated with outward signs in such a manner as to make these distinctly appear as substitutes, or signs equivalent to them.

So far as images act in governing trains of thought and reasoning, they act as signs; but, with reference to the more vivid outward signs, they are, in the animal mind, merged in the things signified, like stars in the light of the sun. Hence, language, in its narrower sense, as the instrument of reflective thought, appears to depend directly on the intensity of significant, or representative, images; since the power to attend to these and intensify them still further, at the same time that an equivalent outward sign is an object of attention, would appear to depend solely on the relative intensities of the two states, or on the relations of intensity in perception and imagination, or in original and revived impressions. The direct power of attention to intensify a revived impression in imagination does not appear to be different in kind from the power of attention in perception, or in outward impressions generally. But this direct power would be obviously aided by the indirect action of attention when fixed by an outward sign, provided attention could be directed to both at the same time; as a single glance may comprehend in one field of view the moon or the brighter planets and the sun, since the moon or planet is not hidden, like the stars, by the glare of day.

As soon, then, as the progress of animal intelligence through an extension of the range in its powers of memory, or in revived impressions, together with a corresponding increase in the vividness of these impressions, has reached a certain point (a progress in itself useful, and therefore likely to be secured in some part of nature, as one among its numerous grounds of selection, or lines of advantage), it becomes possible for such an intelligence to fix its attention on a vivid outward sign, without losing sight of, or dropping out of distinct attention, an image or revived impression; which latter would only serve, in case of its spontaneous revival in imagination, as a sign of the same thing or the same event. Whether the vivid outward sign be a real object or event, of which the revived image is the counterpart, or whether it be a sign in a stricter meaning of the term—that is, some action, figure, or utterance associated either naturally or artificially with all similar objects or events and, consequently, with the revived and representative image of them—whatever the character of this outward sign may be, provided the representative image, or inward sign, still retains, in distinct consciousness, its power as such, then the outward sign may be consciously recognized as a substitute for the inward one, and a consciousness of simultaneous internal and external suggestion, or significance, might be realized; and the contrast of thoughts and things, at least in their power of suggesting that of which they may be coincident signs, could, for the first time, be perceptible. This would plant the germ of the distinctively human form of self-consciousness.

Previously to such a simultaneous consciousness of movements in imagination and movements in the same direction arising from perception, realized through the comparative vividness of the former, all separate and distinct consciousness of the inward sign would be eclipsed, and attention would pass on to the thought suggested by the outward sign. A similar phenomenon is frequently observed with us in successions of inward suggestions, or trains of thought. The attention often skips intermediate steps in a train, or appears to do so. At least, the memory of steps which appear essential to its rational coherency has ceased when we revive the train or repeat it voluntarily. This happens even when only a few moments have elapsed between the train and its repetition. Many writers deny that the omitted steps are immediately forgotten in such cases, on account of their feebleness—as we forget immediately the details of a view which we have just seen, and remember only its salient points; and they maintain that the missing steps are absent from consciousness, even in the original and spontaneous movements of the train, or are present only through an unconscious agency, both in the train and its revival. This being a question of memory, reference cannot be made to memory itself for the decision of it. To decide whether a thing is completely forgotten or has never been experienced, we have no other resource than rational analogy, which, in the present case, appears to favor the theory of oblivion rather than that of latent mental ties and actions, since oblivion is a *vera causa* sufficient to account for the difference between such revived trains and those in which no steps are missed or could be rationally supposed to have been present. The theory of "latent mental agency" appears to confound the original spontaneous movement of the train with what appears as its representative in its voluntary revival. This revival, in some cases, really involves new conditions, and is not, therefore, to be rationally interpreted as a precisely true recollection. If repeated often, it will establish direct and strong associations of contiguity between salient steps in the train which were connected at first by feebler though still conscious steps. The complete obliteration of these is analogous, as I have said, to the loss, in primary forms of memory, of details which are present to consciousness in actual first perceptions.

If, as more frequently happens with us, the whole train, with all its steps of suggestion, is recalled in the voluntary revival of it (without any sense of missing steps), the feebler intermediate links, that in other cases are obliterated, would correspond to the feebler, though (in the more advanced animal intelligences) comparatively vivid, mental signs which have in them the germ, as I have said, of the human form of self-consciousness. The growth of this consciousness, its development from this germ, is a more direct process than the production of the germ itself, which is only incidental to previous utilities in the power of memory. Thought, henceforward, may be an object to thought in its distinct contrast, as an inward sign, with the outward and more vivid sign of that which they both suggest, or revive from memory. This contrast is heightened if the outward one is more strictly a sign, that is, is not the perception of an object or event, of which the inward and representative image is a counterpart, but is of a different nature—for instance, some movement or gesture or vocal utterance, or some graphic sign, associated by contiguity with the object or event, or, more properly, with its representative image. The "concept" so formed is not a thing complete in itself, but is essentially a cause, or step, in mental trains. The outward sign, the image or inward sign, and the suggested thought or image, form a train, like a train which might be wholly within the imagination. This train is present, in all its three constituents, to the first, or immediate, consciousness, in all degrees of intelligence; but in the revival of it, in the inferior degrees of intelligence, the middle term is obliterated, as in the trains of thought above considered. The animal has in mind only an image of the sign, previously present in perception, followed now immediately by an image of what was suggested through the obliterated mental image. But the latter, in the higher degrees of intelligence, is distinctly recalled as a middle term. In the revival of past trains, which were first produced through outward signs, the dumb animal has no consciousness of there having been present more than one of the two successive signs, which, together with the suggested image, formed the actual train in its first occurrence. The remembered outward sign is now a thought, or image, immediately suggesting or recalling that which was originally suggested by a feebler intermediate step. . . .

To exemplify this somewhat abstruse analysis, let us examine what, according to it, would be the mental movements in a man—let him be a sportsman—and a domestic animal—let it be his dog—on hearing a name—let it be the name of some game, as "fox." The general character of the phenomena in both would be the same on the actual first hearing of this word. The word would suggest a mental image of the fox, then its movements of escape from its hunters, and the thought would pass on and dwell, through the absorbing interest of it, on the hunters' movements of pursuit, or pass on even to the capture and destruction of the game. This would, doubtless, recall to the minds of the hunter and his hound one or more real and distinctly remembered incidents of the sort. Now if we suppose this train of thought to be revived (as undoubtedly it is capable of being, both in the man and the dog), it will be the same in the man's mind as on its first production; except that the name "fox" will be thought of (as an auditory, or else a vocal, image) instead of being heard; and the visual image of the fox will be recalled by it with all the succeeding parts of the repeated train. But in the dog, either the auditory image of the name will not be recalled, since the vocal image does not exist in his mind to aid the recall (his voluntary vocal powers not being capable of forming it even in the first instance); or if such an auditory image arises, the representative visual or olfactory [2] one will not appear in distinct consciousness. His attention will pass at once from either of these signs, but from one only to the more intense and interesting parts of the train—to the pursuit and cap-

[2] Images in dogs are supposed to depend largely on the sense of smell.

ture of the game, or to actually remembered incidents of the kind. Either the first or the intermediate sign will remain in oblivion.

Hence the dog's trains of thought, when they are revivals of previous trains, or when they rise into prominent consciousness in consequence of having been passed through before, omit or skip over the steps which at first served only as suggesting and connecting signs, following now only the associations of contiguity, established in the first occurrence of the train, between its more prominent parts. The suggested thought eclipses by its glare the suggesting one. The interest of an image, or its power to attract attention and increased force, depends in the dog only on its vividness as a memory, or as a future purpose or event, and very little, if any, on its relations and agency as a *sign*. Images, as well as outward signs, serve, as I have said, in the dumb animals as well as in man in this capacity; but this is not *recognized* by the animal, since those parts of a train which serve only as signs are too feeble to be revived in the repeated train; and new associations of mere contiguity in the prominent parts of it take their places. All that would be recognized in the animal mind by reflection on thought as thought, or independently of its reality as a memory, an anticipation, or a purpose, would be its unreality, or merely imaginary character.

If, on the contrary, a greater intensity, arising from a greater power of simple memory, should revive the feebler parts in repeated trains of thought to the degree of attracting attention to them and thus bringing them into a more distinct and vivid consciousness, there might arise an interest as to what they are, as to what are their relations, and where they belong, which would be able to inspire and guide an act of distinct reflection. A thought might thus be determined as a representative mental image; and such acts of reflection, inspired also by other motives more powerful than mere inquisitiveness, would by observation, analysis, and generalization (the counterparts of such outward processes in the merely animal mind) bring all such representative images, together with real memories and anticipations, into a single group, or subjective connection. The recognition of them in this connection is the knowledge of them as *my* thoughts, or *our* thoughts, or as phenomena of the mind.

When a thought, or an outward expression, acts in an animal's mind or in a man's in the capacity of a sign, it carries forward the movements of a train and directs attention away from itself to what it signifies or suggests; and consciousness is concentrated on the latter. But being sufficiently vivid in itself to engage distinct attention, it determines a new kind of action and a new faculty of observation, of which the cerebral hemispheres appear to be the organs. From the action of these, in their more essential powers in memory and imagination, the objects or materials of reflection are also derived. Reflection would thus be, not what most metaphysicians appear to regard it, a fundamentally new faculty in man, as elementary and primordial as memory itself, or the power of abstractive attention, or the function of signs and representative images in generalization; but it would be determined in its contrasts with other mental faculties by the nature of its objects. On its subjective side it would be composed of the same mental faculties—namely, memory, attention, abstraction—as those which are employed in the primary use of the senses. It would be engaged upon what these senses have furnished to memory, but would act as independently of any orders of grouping and succession presented by them, as the several senses themselves do of one another. To this extent, reflection is a distinct faculty, and though, perhaps, not peculiar to man, is in him so prominent and marked in its effects on the development of the individual mind that it may be regarded as his most essential and elementary mental distinction in kind. For differences of degrees in causes may make differences of kinds in effects.

Motives more powerful than mere inquisitiveness about the feebler steps or *mere* thoughts of a revived train, and more efficient in concentrating attention upon them and upon their functions as signs, or suggesting images, would spring from the social nature of the animal, from the uses of mental communication between the members of a community, and from the *desire* to communicate which these uses would create. And just as an outward sign associated with a mental image aids by its intensity in fixing attention upon the latter, so the *uses* of such outward signs and the motives connected with their employment would add *extensive* force, or interest, to the energy of attention in the cognition of this inward sign; and hence would aid in the reference of it and its sort to the subject *ego*—a being already known, or distinguished from other beings, as that which wills, desires, and feels. That which wills, desires, and feels is, in the more intelligent domestic animal, known by the proper name, which the animal recognizes and answers to by its actions, and is a consciousness of its individuality. It is not known or recognized by that most generic name "I"; since phenomena common to this individual and to others, or capable of being made common through the communications of language, are not distinctly referred to the individual self by that degree of abstractive attention and precision which an habitual exercise of the faculty of reflection is required to produce. But, in the same manner, the word "world," which includes the conscious subject in its meaning, would fail to suggest anything more to such an intelligence than more concrete terms do—such as what is around, within, and near, and distant from consciousness; or it would fail to suggest the *whole* of that which philosophers divide into *ego* and *nonego,* the outward and inward worlds. A contrast of this whole to its parts, however divided in predication, or the antithesis of subject and attributes, in a divisible unity and its component particulars, would not be suggested to an animal mind by the word "world." . . .

The cognition of the subject world through the distinction in memory of the phenomena of signification from those of outward perception must still be largely aided by the voluntary character of outward signs—vocal, gestural, and graphic—by which all signs are brought under the control of the will, or of that most central, active personality, which is thus connected externally and actively, as well as through the memory, with the inward signs or the representative mental images. These images are brought by this association under stronger and steadier attention; their character, as representative images or signs, is more distinctly seen in reflection, and they are not any longer merely guides in thought, blindly followed. They form, by this association, a little representative world arising to thought at will. Command of language is an important condition of the effective cognition of a sign as such. It is highly probable that the dog not only cannot utter the sound "fox" but cannot revive the sound as heard by him. The word cannot, therefore, be of aid to him in fixing his attention in reflection on the mental image of the fox as seen or smelt by him. But the latter, spontaneously arising, would be sufficient to produce a lively train of thoughts or a vivid dream. It by no means follows from his deficiencies of vocal and auditory imagination that the dog has not, in some directions, aid from outward signs and some small degree of reflective power, though this probably falls far short of the clear division of the two worlds realized in the cognition of *cogito*. Thus he has at command the outward sign of the chase, incipient movements of his limbs such as he makes in his dreams; and this may make the mental image of the chase, with its common obstacles and incidents, distinct in his imagination, in spite of the greater interest which carries the thoughts of his dreams forward to the end of the pursuit, the capture of the game. He may even make use of this sign, as he in fact does when he indicates to his master by his movements his eagerness for a walk or for the chase. . . .

That a dumb animal should not know itself to be a thinking being is hardly more surprising than that it should not be aware of the circulation of its blood and other physiological functions, or that it should not know the anatomy of its frame or that of its nervous system, or the seat of its mental faculties, or the fact that the brain is much smaller in it, in proportion to the size of its body, than in man. Its reflective observation may be as limited in respect to the phenomena of thought as the outward observation of most men is in respect to these results of scientific research. And, on the other hand, the boasted intellectual self-consciousness of man is a knowledge of a subject, not through all its attributes and phenomena, but only through enough of them in general to determine and distinguish it from outward objects and make it serve as the subject of further attributions or predications, as reflective observation makes them known. The abstract forms of this knowledge, the laws of logic and grammar, and the categories of the understanding, which are forms of all scientific knowledge, are all referable to the action of a *purpose* to know and to fix knowledge by precise generalization, just as the mechanical conditions of flight are referable to the purpose to fly and to secure the requisite means. Generalization already exists, however, with particular acts of inquisitiveness in the animal mind; and there is required only the proper degree of attention to signs in order to make it act in accordance with laws which, *if they are universal and necessary laws of the mind,* are equally laws of the animal intelligence, though not actually exemplified in it; just as the laws of locomotion are not actually exemplified in the bodies of plants but are still potential in them.

The inferior and savage races of men, whose languages do not include any abstract terms like truth, goodness, and sweetness, but only concrete ones, like true, good, and sweet, would hardly be able to form a conception, even a vague and obscure one, of the mystic's research of omniscience in the profundities of self-consciousness. They ought on this account, perhaps, to be regarded as races distinct from that of these philosophers, at least mentally, and to be classed, in spite of their powers of speech and limited vocabularies, with the dumb, but still intelligent, animals. If, however, the theory above propounded be true, this greatest of human qualities, intelligent self-consciousness, understood in its actual and proper limits, would follow as a consequence of a greater brain, a greater, or more powerful and vivid memory and imagination, bringing to light, as it were, and into distinct consciousness, phenomena of thought which reflective observation refers to the subject, already known in the dumb animal, or distinguished as an active cause from the forces of outward nature, and from the wills of other animals. The degrees of abstraction and the successively higher and higher steps of generalization, the process which, in scientific knowledge, brings not only the particulars of experience under general designations, but with a conscious purpose brings the less general under the more general, or gives common names not only to each and all resembling objects and relations, but also more general common names to what is denoted by these names, or groups them under higher categories—this process brings together the several forms of self-consciousness. Willing, desiring, feeling, and lastly thinking, also are seen in thought to belong together, or to the same subject; and by thinking they are brought under a common view and receive a common name, or several common names, to wit, "my mind," "me," "I," "my mental states." . . .

Not only the dog and other intelligent dumb animals, but some of the least advanced among human beings, also, are unable to arrive at a distinct abstraction of what is expressed by "to be" or "to exist." Being is concreted, or determined, to such minds down, at least, to the conception of living or acting, to a conception scarcely above what is implied in the actions of the more intelligent animals, namely, their apprehension of themselves as agents or patients with wills and feelings distinct from those of other animals, and from the forces and interests of outward nature generally. "Your dog is here, or is coming, and at your service," is a familiar expression in the actions of dogs not remarkable for intelligence. A higher degree of abstraction and generalization than the simple steps, which are sufficient, as we have seen, for inference in enthymematic reasonings to particular conclusions, would be required in reflection; and a more extensive and persistent exercise of the faculty of reflection, aided by voluntary signs or by language, than any dumb animal attains to, would be needed to arrive at the cognition of *cogito* and *sum*. This is a late acquisition with children; and it would, indeed, be surprising if the mind of a dumb animal should attain to it. But there is little ground in this for believing, with most metaphysicians, that the cognition is absolutely *sui generis*, or an ultimate and underived form of knowledge; or that it is not approached gradually, as well as realized with different degrees of clearness and precision, as the faculty of reflection becomes more and more exercised.[3]

[The Metaphysics of Self-Consciousness] [4]

The world of self-conscious intellectual activity—the world of mind—has, doubtless, its ultimate unconditional laws, everywhere exemplified in the actual phenomena of abstractive and reflective thought, and capable of being generalized in the reflective observations of the philosopher and applied by him to the explanation of the phenomena of thought wherever manifested in outward expressions, whether in his fellow men or in the more intelligent dumb animals. Memory, in the effects of its more powerful and vivid revivals with the more intelligent animals, and especially in the case of large-brained man, presents this new world, in which the same faculties of observation, analysis, and generalization as those employed by intelligent beings in general, ascertain the marks and classes of phenomena strictly mental, and divide them, as a whole class or *summum genus*, from those of the outward world. The distinction of subject and object becomes thus a classification through observation and analysis instead of the intuitive distinction it is supposed to be by most metaphysicians. Intuitive to some extent, in one sense of the word, it doubtless is; that is, facilities and predispositions to associations, which are as effective as repeated experiences and observations would be, and which are inherited in the form of instincts, doubtless have much to do in bringing to pass this cognition, as well as many others, which appear to be innate, not only in the lower animals but also in man. . . . Such a reference of the distinction of subject and object to instinctive tendencies in our minds is not equivalent to the metaphysical doctrine that this distinction is intuitive. For

[3] [This last paragraph is printed out of order for expository purposes.]
[4] [*North American Review*, CXVI (1873), 264-265, 274-284.]

this implies more than is meant by the word "instinctive" from the naturalist's point of view. It implies that the cognition is absolute, independent not only of the individual's experiences but of all possible previous experience, and has a certainty, reality, and cogency that no amount of experience could give to an empirical classification.

The metaphysical dogmas, for which this formula is given, deserve but a passing scientific consideration. Truths independent of all experience are not known to exist, unless we exclude from what we mean by "experience" that which we have in learning the meanings of words and in agreeing to definitions and the conventions of language—excluding these truths or identical propositions on the ground that they depend solely, or may be considered as depending solely, on a lexical authority, from which a kind of necessity comes independent of reality in the relations and connections of the facts denoted by the words. It is possible that laws exist absolutely universal, binding fate and infinite power as well as speech and the intelligible use of words; but it is not possible that the analytical processes of any finite intellect should discover what particular laws these are. Such an intellect may legislate with absolute freedom in the realm of definition and word-making, provided it limits itself to its autonomy and does not demand of other intellects that they shall be governed by such laws on account of the universal applications of them in the world of common experience. It is also possible that beliefs or convictions may exist, believed by the mystic to be independent of all ordinary forms of particular experience, "which no amount of experience could produce"; but it is not true that there are any universal or scientific beliefs of this kind. The effects of inherited aptitudes, and of early, long-continued, and constantly repeated experiences in the individual, together with the implications of language itself, in fixing and in giving force and certainty to an idea or a belief, have, probably, not been sufficiently considered by those metaphysicians who claim a preternatural and absolute origin for certain of our cognitions; or else, perhaps, the more dogmatic among these thinkers overestimate the force and certainty of the beliefs, or mistake the *kind* of necessity they have. The essential importance, the necessity and universality in language, of pronominal words or signs, should not be mistaken for a real a priori necessity in the relations expressed by them. Metaphysicians should consider that *ego* and *nonego*, as real existences, are not individual phenomena but groups with demonstrative names the least possible determined in meaning, or are the most abstract subjects of the phenomena of experience, though determined, doubtless, in their applications partly by spontaneous, instinctive, or natural and inherited tendencies to their formation.

This view of the origin of the cognition of *cogito* is equally opposed to the schemes of "idealism" and "natural realism," which divide modern schools of philosophy. According to the "idealists," the conscious subject is immediately known, at least in its phenomena, and the phenomena are intuitively known to belong to it; while the existence of anything external to the mind is an inference from the phenomena of self, or a reference of some of them to external causes. Objects are only known mediately "by their effects on *us*." Against this view the "natural realist" appeals effectively to the common-sense or natural judgment of unsophisticated minds, and is warranted by this judgment in declaring that the object of consciousness is *just as immediately* known as the subject is. But natural realism goes beyond this judgment and holds that both the subject and object are absolutely, immediately, and equally known through their essential attributes in perception. This is more than an unlearned jury are competent to say. For if by immediacy we mean the relation which a particular *unattributed* phenomenon has to consciousness in general, we are warranted in saying that immediately, or without the step of attribution, subject and object are undistinguished in consciousness. Thus the sensations of sound and color and taste and pleasure and pain, and the emotions of hope and fear and love and hate, *if not yet referred to their causes, or even classified as sensations and emotions*, belong to neither world exclusively. But so far as any man can remember, no such unattributed or unclassified states of consciousness are experienced. He cannot say, however, that they cannot exist, or (what is worse for the theory) be wrongly attributed or classified. All states of consciousness are, it is true, referred to one or the other, or partly to each of the two worlds; and this attribution is, in part at least, instinctive, yet not independent of all experience, since it comes either from the direct observation of our progenitors or, possibly, through the natural selection of them—that is, possibly through the survival of those who rightly divided the worlds, and did not often mistake a real danger for a dream or for an imagined peril, nor often mistake a dream of security for real safety. If, however, we mean by immediacy such an instinctive attribution, independent of repeated connections of attributes in their subject through the individual's own experiences, then "natural realism" is most in accordance with our view, or with such exceptions as the mistakes and corrections of dreams and hallucinations imply, and excepting the ontological or metaphysical positions that are assumed in it.

If the natural realist is not also an evolutionist (and usually he is not), then his meaning of intuitions must be that they are absolute and underived universal facts of connection in phenomena. He must suppose that distinct phenomena have stamped upon them indelible marks of their ultimate highest class, equivalents for "I" and "not-I," as the individuals of a herd of cattle are branded with the mark of their owner. Such an immutable mark would, however, render the mistakes of insanity, hallucinations, and dreams impossible, or else would refer them (as has actually been supposed [5]) to the mystery of the existence of evil—a convenient disposition of philosophical puzzles. In the doctrine of evolution the meaning of the word "intuition" does not imply immutability in the connections of instinctively combined phenomena, except where such connection is an ultimate law of nature or is the simplest causal connection, like the laws of motion or the laws of logic (regarding logic as a science, and not merely as an art). The intuition of space in the blind might be, from this point of view, a differ-

[5] Dr. McCosh, *On the Intuitions of the Mind.*

ent combination of sensibilities from that in other men; and the interpretation of sensations of hearing or sight in hallucinations as being caused by outward objects—when in reality they arise from disturbances or abnormal conditions of the nervous system—would not be an interpretation involving violations of ultimate laws, or suspensions in rebellious Nature of relations between cause and effect. Variations in intuitions and instinctive judgments would be as natural and explicable as errors of judgment are in the experiences of the individual man. But the doctrine of natural realism, independently of that of evolution and the implied mutability of instincts, has insurmountable difficulties.

Idealism, on the other hand, appears to contradict not the abnormal so much as the common phenomena of consciousness. It appears to be related to the modern sciences of physics and physiology very nearly as natural realism is to scholastic logic and ontology. Dating from the time of Descartes, it appears, in all its forms, to depend on a more exact knowledge of the bodily apparatus and outward physical causes of perception than the ancients possessed. By these researches it appeared that perception, and even sensation, is fully determined or realized in the brain only through other parts of the bodily apparatus, and through outward forces and movements like those of pressure and vibration. That the perception, or sensation, is experienced, or is seated, in the brain was a natural and proper conclusion from these researches. That the apparent object of perception is not only distant from what thus appeared to be the seat of the perception, but that a long series of usually unknown, or unnoticed, movements intervenes between it and this apparent seat—these facts gave great plausibility to a confused interpretation of the phenomena, namely, that the perception is first realized as a state of the conscious *ego*, and, afterwards, is referred to the outward world through the associations of general experience, as an effect produced upon us by an otherwise unknown outward cause. On similar grounds a similar misinterpretation was made of the phenomena of volition, namely, that a movement in ourselves, originally and intuitively known to be *ours*, produces an effect in the outward world at a distance from us through the intervention of a series of usually unknown (or only indirectly known) agencies. Remote effects of the outer world on us, and our actions in producing remote effects on it, appeared to be the first or intuitive elements in our knowledge of these phenomena, all the rest being derived or inferential. This was to confound the seat of sensation or perception in the brain with its proper subjectivity, or the reference of it to the subject.

The position in the brain where the last physical condition for the production of a sensation is situated is, no doubt, properly called the place or seat of the sensation, especially as it is through the movements of the brain with other special nervous tracts, and independently of any movements out of the nervous system, that like sensations are, or can be, revived, though these revived ones are generally feebler than those that are set in movement by outward forces. Nevertheless, this physiological seat of a sensation is no part of our direct knowledge of it. A priori we cannot assign it any place, nor decide that it has, or has not, a place. The place which we do assign it, in case it is outward, is the place determined by a great variety of sensations and active forms of consciousness experienced in the localization of the object to which it is referred. It is only by the association (either spontaneous and instinctive, or acquired) of this sensation with those sensations and actions that are involved in the localization of the object that we arrive at any notion of its locality. If we do not form any such associations of it with otherwise determined localities, and if it and its kind remain after much experience unlocalized or only vaguely localized in our bodies, it is then, *but not till then,* referred to the conscious self as a subjective phenomenon. There remains the alternative, of course, in the theory of evolution, that the negative experiences which would thus determine the subjective character of a phenomenon may be the experiences of our progenitors, and that our judgment of this character may be, in many cases, an instinctive one, arising from the inherited effects of these former experiences. Otherwise this judgment in the individual mind, and from its own experiences, would appear to be posterior, in point of time, to its acquaintance with the object world, since this judgment would be determined by the *absence* of any uniform connection in the phenomenon with the phenomena of locality. Instead of being, as the theories of idealism hold, first known as a phenomenon of the subject *ego*, or as an effect upon us of an hypothetical outward world, its first unattributed condition would be, by our view, one of neutrality between the two worlds.

In dissenting, therefore, from both extremes—the theory of idealism and that of natural realism, or assenting to the latter only as qualified by the theory of evolution—I have supposed both theories to be dealing with the two worlds only as worlds of phenomena, without considering the metaphysical bearings and varieties of them with respect to the question of the cognition of nonphenomenal existences, on the grounds of belief in an inconceivable and metaphysical matter or spirit; for, according to the view proposed as a substitute for these extremes, subject and object are only names of the highest classes, and are not the names of inconceivable substrata of phenomena. Ontology or metaphysics would not be likely to throw much original light on the scientific evolution of self-consciousness; but it becomes itself an interesting object of study as a phase of this evolution seen in the light of science. When one comes to examine in detail the supposed cognitions of supersensible existences, and the faculty of necessary truth which is called "the reason," or else is described in its supposed results as the source of necessary beliefs or convictions, or of natural and valid hypotheses of inconceivable realities, great difficulty is experienced, on account of the abstract character of the beliefs, in distinguishing what is likely to be strictly inherited from what is early and uniformly acquired in the development of the faculty of reflection, and especially from what is imbibed through language, the principal philosophical instrument of this faculty. The languages employed by philosophers are themselves lessons in ontology, and have, in their grammatical structures, implied conceptions and beliefs common to the philosopher and to the barbarian inventors of language, as well as other implications which he takes pains to avoid. How much besides he ought to avoid, in the correction of conceptions erroneously taken from the forms of language, is a question always important to be considered in metaphysical inquiries.

The conception of *substance*, as a nature not fully involved in the contrast of essential and accidental attributes, and the connection, or coexistence, of them in our experiences, or the conception of it as also implying the real, though latent, coexistence of all attributes in an existence unknown to us, or known only in a nonphenomenal and inconceivable way—this conception needs to be tested by an examination of the possible causes of it as an effect of the forms of language and other familiar associations, which, however natural, may still be misleading. To the minds of the barbarian inventors of language, words had not precise meanings, for definition is not a barbarian accomplishment. Hence, to such minds, definite and precise attributions, as of sweetness to honey and sugar, or light to the day, to the heavenly bodies, or to fire, are strongly in contrast with the vagueness which appears to them inherent in substantive names—inherent not as vagueness, however, but as *something else.* Such names did not clearly distinguish persons and things, for the day and the heavenly bodies were personal, and fire apparently was an animal or a spirit. Removing as much as possible of mere crudeness from such conceptions, predication would yet appear to be a reference of something distinctly known to something essentially unknown, or known only by one or a few attributes needed to distinguish it by a name, as proper names distinguish persons. The meaning of this name, and the conception of it as meaning much more, and as actually referring to unapparent powers of bringing to light attributes previously unknown—powers manifested in an actual effect when a new attribute is added in predication—this vague, ill-defined, and essentially hidden meaning is assimilated in grammar, and thence in philosophy, to an agent putting forth a new manifestation of itself in a real self-assertion.

The contrast of "active and passive" in the forms of verbs illustrates how the barbaric mind mounted into the higher regions of abstraction in language through concrete imaginations. The subject of a proposition, instead of being thought as that vaguely determined group of phenomena with which the predicate is found to be connected, was thought either to perform an action on an object through the transitive verb, or to be acted on by the object through the passive form, or to put forth an action absolute, expressed by the neuter verb, or to assert its past, present, or future existence absolutely, and its possession of certain properties by the substantive verb, and by the copula and predicate. This personification of the subject of a proposition, which is still manifested in the forms and terminology of grammar, is an assimilation of things to an active, or at least demonstrative, self-consciousness or personality. It had hardly reached the degree of abstraction needed for the clear intellectual self-consciousness of *cogito*. It rather implied that things also think. The invention of substantive names for attributes, that is, abstract names like goodness or truth—an invention fraught with most important consequences to human knowledge—brought at first more prominently forward the realistic tendencies which philosophers have inherited from the barbarian inventors of language. Abstract names do not appear to have been meant at first to be the direct names of attributes or collections of attributes, as "goodness" and "humanity," but to be the names of powers (such as make things good, or make men what they are), which appear to be results of the earliest conscious or scientific analysis in the progress of the human mind, but names strongly tainted still by the barbaric conception of words as the names of active beings. Abstract words were not, however, as active or demonstrative as their savage progenitors, the concrete general substantives. They appear rather as artificers, or the agents which build up things, or make them what they are. But, by means of them, concrete general names were deprived of their powers and reduced to subjection. To have direct general names, and to have general powers, appear to be synonymous to savage and semibarbarous minds.

I have spoken as if all this were a matter of past history instead of being an actually present state of philosophical thought and a present condition of some words in the minds of many modern thinkers. The misleading metaphors are, it is true, now recognized as metaphors; but their misleading character is not clearly seen to its full extent. The subjects of propositions are still made to do the work, to bear the impositions, to make known the properties and accidents expressed by their predicates, or to assert their own existence and autonomy, just so far as they are supposed to be the names of anything but the assemblages of known essential qualities or phenomena actually coexistent in our experiences—the qualities which their definitions involve, and to which other attributes are added (but from which they are not evolved) in real predication—or just so far as they are supposed to be the names of unknown and imperceptible entities. Names are directly the designations of things, not of hidden powers, or wills, in things. But it is not necessary to regard them as precisely definable, or as connoting definite groups of qualities or the essential attributes of things, in order that they may fulfill the true functions of words; for they are still only the names of things, not of wills in things, on one hand, nor of "concepts" or thoughts in us, on the other hand. They are synonyms of "concepts," if we please to extend synonymy so as to include the whole range of the *signs* of things; but both the "concept" and its verbal synonym may be, and generally are, *vague.* For just as in the major premises of syllogisms the subject is, in general, a codesignation of two undivided parts of a class of objects, one known directly to have, or lack, the attributes affirmed or denied in this premise, and the other part, judged by induction to be also possessed, or not possessed, of them—a codesignation in which the conclusion of the syllogism is virtually contained, so as to make the syllogism appear to be a *petitio principii* (as it would be but for this implied induction [6])—so in the simple naming of objects the names may be properly regarded as the names of groups of qualities, in which groups the qualities are partly known and partly

[6] See Mill's *Logic,* B. II, ch. 3.

unknown, predication in real (not verbal) propositions being the conversion of the latter into the former. But in this view of the functions of words, it is necessary, at least, to suppose enough of the known attributes of objects is involved in the meanings of their names to make the applications of the names distinct and definite. Names, with the capacity they would thus acquire, or have actually had, in spite of metaphysics, of having their meanings modified or changed, are best adapted to the functions of words in promoting the progress of knowledge. From this use of words their essences, both the apparent and the inscrutable, have disappeared altogether, except so far as the actual existence and coexistence of the known attributes of objects are implied by names, or so far as the coexistence of these with previously unknown ones is also implied by the use of names as the subjects of propositions. No inscrutable powers in words or things, nor any immutable connections among the attributes called essential, are thus imposed upon the use of words in science.

Metaphysicians, on the other hand, in nearly all that is left to the peculiar domain of their inquiries, possess their problems and solutions in certain words, such as "substance," "cause," "matter," "mind," still retaining, at least with them, the barbaric characters we have examined. Matter and mind still retain, not only with metaphysicians, but also with the vulgar, designations of unknown inscrutable powers in the outward and inward worlds, or powers which, according to some, are known only to a higher form of intuition through the faculty of "Reason"; or, being really inscrutable and inconceivable by any human faculty, as others hold, they are, nevertheless, regarded as certainly existent, and attested by irresistible natural beliefs. That beliefs in beings, unknown and unknowable, are real beliefs, and are natural (though more so to some minds than to others), seems a priori probable on the theory of evolution, without resorting to the effects of early training and the influence of associations in language itself, by which the existence of such beliefs is accounted for by some scientific philosophers. But the authority which the theory of evolution would assign to these beliefs is that of the conceptions which barbarous and vulgar minds have formed of the functions of words, and of the natures which they designate. Inheritance of these conceptions, that is, of aptitudes or tendencies to their formation, and the continued action of the causes so admirably analyzed by Mr. Mill,[7] through which he proposes to account for those beliefs directly, and which have retained, especially in the metaphysical conception of "matter," the barbarian's feelings and notions about real existence as a power to produce phenomena, are sufficient to account for the existence of these beliefs and their cogency, without assigning them any force as authorities. . . .

[AN EMPIRICIST ANALYSIS OF SPACE]

To Mr. Abbot[1]

Cambridge, June 26, 1865.
Cambridge, July 9, 1867.

I trust you will not consider the long time I have allowed to pass before responding to your friendly challenge to a philosophical tournament as any indication of hesitation or unwillingness on my part to undertake the correspondence you propose. I had much rather you would regard it as time required to consider the difficult problems—involving, as they do, so many knotty points and grounds of diverse opinions; but in fact the time has not been so employed. I have had few opportunities and fewer occasions of inspiration; and nothing but comparative leisure at present and a desire to express the pleasure and gratification I received from your letter and your request for further correspondence excuses the present attempt to respond to them.

The clear summary which you give of your argument for the infinity of space, and the questions which you propose as con-

[7] See Mill's *Examination of Hamilton,* ch. 11.

[1] [This section is drawn from two sources: *Letters,* pp. 76-82, 103-106.]

taining the chief issues between us, help me to bring my thoughts at once to the discussion. You ask first, "What is the origin of the idea of space simply considered, as the absolute correlate and condition of matter irrespective of its infinity?" In answer, I propose to give, as briefly as I can, the empiricist's interpretation of the admitted facts of space, and his explanation of what he conceives to be the origin of the idea. "The idea of space as the *necessary and absolute condition* of matter," as "the *receptacle of matter*, without which as an extended object it could not exist," includes, it seems to me, a confusion of two distinct propositions, on the discrimination of which the empiricist bases his criticism of the absolutist's philosophy. He denies that any necessity is cognizable except the necessities of thought; and he would consequently say of the idea of space that though it is necessary to the representation of matter as an object of thought, yet it cannot be known as the necessary and absolute condition of matter per se or as underlying noumenal existence. Things and their relations known as phenomena, and their laws, include all that is known to us, except bare existence. Space and Time, distinctly known by abstraction and generalization, are none the less relations of things, merely because they are the absolute conditions [of thinking] of things, the *conditio sine qua non* of their existence [to us]. And there is not any true or unavoidable antithesis between "abstractions, generalizations, or relations" and the "absolute correlates of things" as thought. Relations may be necessary as well as contingent; and because things cannot be conceived out of certain relations, it does not follow that these relations have any other existence than in the things in which they are cognized. To postulate the order, which experience determines in our thinking, as also the order of ontological dependence, is to assume at once and without adequate discussion the position against which the empiricist protests.

The conception of Time and Space as primarily any other than those relations which are universal in our experience of things comes from confounding the truly abstract Time and Space with their abstract representations. I mean by abstract representation the imaging in the fantasy of as few of the properties and relations of sensible objects as can be represented, excluding or leaving in the background all else. Such syntheses of all the relations necessary to the conception of things in general give the abstract ideas of space as the "receptacle of matter" and of time as the continuum of events. These are not primary intuitions, but constructive synthetic representations made up of the elementary abstract relations of things and events. What we really and immediately know are phenomena—objects and events—with their relations. Proceeding to know them better and better, we first class them by the ultimate and truly unanalyzable principle of "likeness and unlikeness." Resemblances and differences of all degrees are cognized, and those phenomena in which resemblance is as perfect as is consistent with their plurality are still found to differ in what we call Space and Time; and this is all we ultimately know of space and time. They are the abstract genera of differences which exist between all phenomena as plural, however great resemblances they may have. An identical object is known by phenomena differing in time only. The universality of the relations of space and time in our experience, and their consequent necessity in our thoughts, united with the notion of identity in an object, gives the notion of *continuity of existence* both in space and time. We are not immediately cognizant of this continuity as such. What we know are discrete phenomena and their relations of resemblance and difference.

I do not believe that Space and Time are pure hypotheses posited to account for the relations of phenomena. I think they are really cognized as ultimate differences in phenomena; but the continuities of Space and Time must either be of the nature of hypotheses or else I think we must grant your position of a faculty above sense and understanding capable of cognizing them. As hypotheses and as the only hypotheses we can form to account for or rationalize our experiences, they may be regarded as truly necessary to thought and universal, like the relations on which they are founded.

That time continues between any two events, and that space

extends between any two objects cognized by us, is inferred as being simply necessary to thought, since we cannot imagine any quantitative difference which is not divisible nor any parts which are not different in space and time. The relations of space and time are intuitions of sense; but as receptacle and continuum, or as conditions of these relations, they are hypotheses. The conception of continuity involves that of quantity, which I think is primarily cognized as a relation of the relations of time and space—and, I may add, of intension in sensation or power. Two events are conceived quantitatively as separated by other events or the possibility of other events which still differ in time. And similarly of objects in space and of sensations. Objects, events, and feelings are related in space, time, and power, and these are related in quantity. Out of the vague apprehension of quantitative relations in these, we form precise abstract conceptions of quantity, which we cannot however separate entirely from these relations. We have therefore three species of quantity—quantity in space, time, and degree.

But you may object that a rationalizing hypothesis, which, you will say, is not, and cannot be, given by sense or understanding, must come from a faculty above these, which is also the source of the validity of the hypothesis; but I contend that so far as such an hypothesis is apprehended at all, and so far as it has any validity, it is apprehended and vouched for by understanding and sense. The process is perfectly analogous to the formation of general ideas, which it is now admitted on all hands cannot be apprehended by sense or represented in imagination, yet is the proper function of understanding dealing with the data of experience. In the same way, the hypothesis of a receptacle or continuum, so far as it is apprehended at all, is apprehended in and through the relations of the phenomena which it reduces to rational order. As well contend that mathematical formulas and processes which convey no meaning in themselves, but develop implicit relations of quantity, are given and vouched for by a special faculty, as contend that space—the receptacle—is a distinct datum of intelligence.

The distinction between Space and Extension is thus to my mind only that which subsists between an abstract synthetic hypothesis and the elementary relations which it reduces to order and harmony in thought. The latter alone are properly apprehended by any faculty of knowledge. Space is really apprehended in the relations of extension in bodies. All bodies—the whole nonego of sense, embraced in one intuition, with the exclusion of all which is nonessential to representation in general—give us the space of imagination. Rational space is that which is essential to clear, distinct, and rational thought, or is necessary to understanding. It excludes color and tangible properties, and includes the hypothesis of continuity. Sense by itself does not give continuity, but at the same time does not exclude it. All the data of sense are in accordance with it; and hence they verify or give validity to it, so far as it has validity or is capable of verification. The impossibility of thinking contrary to it is not regarded by the empiricist as a distinct kind of proof. This only expresses the degree of the proof which experience affords.

I come now to your question concerning the infinity of space. This predication, though it cannot be understood, cannot be denied, since it involves no contradiction. At the same time, it cannot be affirmed as an hypothesis necessary to account for any cognizable fact which is not accounted for by the idea "that space extends beyond our powers of knowing or conceiving it." What infinite space includes, more than this, is unnecessary, and therefore unwarranted; and it is only by sublating the contradictory proposition [that space is limited], as you propose to do in your proof, that it can be posited.

But what is the contradictory of infinite space as distinguished from indefinite space? Not finite space simply, as you propose in your proof. The truly infinite is the unconditionally unlimited or indefinite, and its contradictory is the unconditionally limited—not merely the finite, which may be conditionally limited. What you really sublate in your proof is only the conditionally limited as predicated of abstract space. You say: "For suppose it [space] limited, it must be limited either by matter or by vacuity [that is in either case conditionally limited]; but Space is presupposed by matter, and is itself, in the absence of matter, vacuity, consequently, etc."

But this dilemma does not include an alternative which is the real contradictory of infinite space. Unconditionally limited space is neither limited by other space nor by matter, but per se or by itself. This is inconceivable, of course—obtrusively and staggeringly so—but it does not involve any logical contradiction, and is not therefore repugnant to reason any more than its equally inconceivable contradictory, infinite space.

Since therefore I must disallow your demonstration of infinity, I come to your third question, "What is the reason why the infinity of space is a less obtrusive and staggering inconceivability than its [absolute] finitude?"

[I should say] that "we finally rest on unlimited space as the least obtrusive and staggering inconceivability, [since it is] the one for which we can most easily substitute a pseud representation, namely, an indefinitely great extension." The suffering senses are quieter, but the understanding is still frustrated. Aesthetic considerations—or perhaps I should say *anaesthetic* considerations—decide, where reason is balanced. The decision is the other way—and for the same reason—in the case of the infinite and absolute of causation. An absolute beginning is preferable to an infinite nonbeginning, because we can easily substitute for it a pseud representation, namely, a beginning in knowledge or in consciousness, which, in the case of our own volitions, seem like new creations, self-determined. This satisfies sense and imagination by deceiving them, but the understanding is still baffled.

Infinite space, as an hypothesis to account for anything of which we are truly cognizant, not only transcends our powers of conception but also the necessities of thought. A simpler hypothesis is competent to do all that it can do. We need only space which includes all that we can know, and extends beyond our powers of knowing or conceiving it. . . .

You infer from my exposition of the empiricist's doctrine of space and time that I "deny them all *independent* objective existence." I would modify a little this deduction. I regard them as objects—phenomenal objects—and not merely as forms of sensibility. As to their "*independent* objective" (if you mean by this, noumenal) existence, I can deny or affirm nothing—only that space and time, as we know them, and, consequently, as they are to us, are relations among phenomena; and, as we know, they depend, or "are conditioned on the existence of phenomena themselves." Your conclusion, that "could we conceive the annihilation of phenomena, the relations subsisting between them would also be annihilated," is, therefore, in substance, correctly deduced, though it should be more explicitly stated that the phenomena and the relations here spoken of are also "conditioned on the existence" of a knowing mind; and that the annihilation supposed is the annihilation of thought as well as of its object. What would remain we know nothing about. Things in themselves and their relations to one another, whether real or not, are not real to us—are not objects of our knowledge; though, if they exist, they may be the causes of our knowledge.

I assent also to your inference that, in my opinion, "relations are objective realities"; but I would not be understood as allowing by this that I regard them as noumenal realities. Whether the latter exist, and whatever they may be, the relations of which we are treating are relations of objects, which are only known as objects to us, and as conditioned on our cognizance of them. I believe that the relations between such objects belong to them—are objective—and are not molds or forms in us into which objects fit.

When I spoke of the relations of time and space as "intuitions of sense," I ought, perhaps, to have explained that I did not hold the abstract cognizance of them as possible in sensuous or, indeed, in any other intuition. Such cognizance implies, it seems to me, the abstractive action of the attention in understanding—not any intuitive power at all. More correctly, I should have said that the grounds of relations (*fundamenta relationum*) are intuitions of sense; the relations themselves, as distinct from their concrete terms, being cognizable, not intuitively, but only by abstraction, and being representable only by the reproduction of such and so many sensuous data as are implied in them. The cognizance of relations is, indeed, an abstractive grouping of phenomena. The *twoness* of two hats (to take your example) is as much in the hats as their color, texture, or form; but the cognizance of it in the abstract is not an intuitive process at all. It adds no content to the concrete cognizance of the group. It subtracts rather the texture, form, use, and all other attributes of the manifold object—leaving to our attention only difference in space and a species of plurality, which, by similar acts, we have generalized under the name of "two." I, "who admit the objectivity of relations, and hold them to be *immediately* known [in the concrete], can deny that here is logically necessitated a higher intuitive faculty than sense," because to me intuition signifies a concrete addition to the content of our cognitions. I admit that space, time, and number are peculiar—unlike most other apparently simple notions which we generalize from the manifold of sensuous intuitions. They are not referable to simple and unanalyzable sensations, such as give us the color and texture of the hats; nor are they analyzable into a plurality of simpler relations, such as is implied in the *use* of the hats. They resemble the latter notion in being distinctly cognizable only by abstraction. They resemble sensations in being apparently simple. It may be admitted, until an analysis has been proposed, that number, and perhaps also time, are simple, unanalyzable properties of things in general *as objects of knowledge*. That they appear only in acts of abstraction and understanding does not prove, however, that they are intuitions of a supersensuous faculty, unless it can be shown that the understanding adds as well as subtracts in its discursions.

With space, the case is different. Our apprehension of it may in one way be analyzed. Introspective analysis cannot, it is true, resolve it into simpler elements; but we can easily conceive of it as an *idea of sensation* (as Locke called it), as consisting of an unanalyzable group of sensations cemented by insoluble associations. On this hypothesis, the universality of space in our cognitions comes from its invariable association with other and really simpler sensations, and its simplicity comes from the limit in our powers of introspective analysis. . . .

IV

COSMOLOGY

[CRITIQUE OF THE NEBULAR HYPOTHESIS] [1]

In 1811 Sir William Herschel [2] communicated to the Royal Society a paper in which he gave an exposition of his famous hypothesis of the transformation of nebulae into stars. "Assuming a self-luminous substance of a highly attenuated nature to be distributed through the celestial regions, he endeavored to show that, by the mutual attraction of its constituent parts, it would have a tendency to form itself into distinct aggregations of nebulous matter, which in each case would gradually condense from the continued action of the attractive forces, until the resulting mass finally acquired the consistency of a solid body, and became a star. In those instances wherein the collection of nebulous matter was very extensive, subordinate centres of attraction could not fail to be established, around which the adjacent particles would arrange themselves; and thus the whole mass would in process of time be transformed into a determinate number of discrete bodies, which would ultimately assume the condition of a cluster of stars. Herschel pointed out various circumstances which appeared to him to afford just grounds for believing that such a nebulous substance existed independently in space. He maintained that the phenomena of nebulous stars, and the changes observable in the great nebula of Orion, could not be satisfactorily accounted

1 [From "A Physical Theory of the Universe," *North American Review*, XCIX (1864), 1-11.]

2 [Sir John F. W. Herschel (1792-1871), English astronomer and philosopher of science, constructed in 1820, for a reflecting telescope, a mirror of 18 inches diameter and 20 feet focal length, which enabled him to make the astronomical observations on which his fame was mainly based.]

for by any other hypothesis. Admitting, then, the existence of a nebulous substance, he concluded, from indications of milky nebulosity which he encountered in the course of his observations, that it was distributed in great abundance throughout the celestial regions. The vast collections of nebulae which he had observed, of every variety of structure and in every stage of condensation, were employed by him with admirable address in illustrating the *modus operandi* of his hypothesis." [3]

Laplace,[4] in his *Système du monde,* applied this hypothesis, by an ingenious but simple use of mechanical principles, to the explanation of the origin of the planetary bodies, and of the general features of their movements in the solar system. Supposing the original nebulous mass to receive a rotatory motion by its aggregation, he showed that this motion would be quickened by a further contraction of the mass, until the centrifugal force of its equatorial regions would be sufficient to balance their gravitation, and to suspend them in the form of a vaporous ring. Again, supposing this revolving ring to be broken, and finally collected by a further aggregation into a spherical nebulous mass, he showed, in the same way, how the body of a planet, with its system of satellites, might be formed. The material and the original motions of the planets and their satellites could thus, he supposed, be successively produced, as the nebula gradually contracted to the dimensions of the sun.

No scientific theory has received a fairer treatment than the nebular hypothesis. Arising as it did as a speculative conclusion from one of the grandest inductions in the whole range of physical inquiry—connecting as it does so many facts, though vaguely and inconclusively, into one system—it possesses, what is rare in so bold and heterodox a view, a verisimilitude quite disproportionate to the real evidence which can be adduced

[3] Grant's *History of Physical Astronomy.*

[4] [Laplace, Pierre Simon, Marquis de (1749-1827), French mathematician and astronomer, wrote *Mécanique célèste, Exposition du système du monde* —where his famous nebular hypothesis, which Wright constantly criticized, appeared as a note—and *Théorie analytique des probabilités*—where he propounded the "classical" theory of probability.]

in its support. The difficulties which ordinarily attend the reception of new ideas were in this case removed beforehand. The hypothesis violated no habitual association of ideas, at least among those who were at all competent to comprehend its import. Though resting on a much feebler support of direct evidence than the astronomical theories of Copernicus, Galileo, and Kepler,[5] it met with a cordial reception from its apparent accordance with certain preconceptions of the same kind as those which, though extrinsic and irrelevant to scientific inquiry, were able to oppose themselves successfully for a long time to the ascertained truths of modern astronomy.

The test of conceivableness, the receptivity of the imagination, is a condition, if not of truth itself, at least of belief in the truth; and in this respect the nebular hypothesis was well founded. It belonged to that class of theories of which it is sometimes said "that, if they are not true, they *deserve* to be true." A place was already prepared for it in the imaginations and the speculative interests of the scientific world.

We propose to review briefly some of the conditions which have given so great a plausibility to this hypothesis. In the first place, on purely speculative grounds, this hypothesis, as a cosmological theory, happily combines the excellences of the two principal doctrines on the origin of the world that were held by the ancients, and which modern theorists have discussed as views which, though neither can be established scientifically, have no less interest from a theological point of view: namely,

[5] [Nicolaus Copernicus (1473-1543), Polish astronomer, advanced his revolutionary heliocentric theory in his great work, *Concerning the Revolutions of the Celestial Spheres*.

Galileo Galilei (1564-1642), Italian physicist and astronomer, espoused the Copernican System and laid the foundations, both logically and experimentally, of modern science. Galileo's masterpieces are *A Dialogue on the Two Principal Systems of the World* (1632) and *Dialogues on the Two New Sciences* (1636).

Johannes Kepler (1571-1630), German mathematician and astronomer, formulated the laws of planetary motion. For an analysis of the astronomical concepts of these three important thinkers, cf. Chapter 2 of *Theories of Scientific Method from the Renaissance to the Nineteenth Century*, R. W. Blake, C. J. Ducasse, and E. H. Madden.]

first, the materialistic doctrine that the world, though finite in the duration of its orderly successions and changes, is infinite in the duration of its material substance; and, secondly, the spiritualistic doctrine, that matter and form are equally the effects, finite in duration, of a spiritual and eternal cause.

At first sight the nebular hypothesis seems to agree most nearly with the materialistic cosmology as taught by the greater number of the ancient philosophers; but the resemblance is only superficial, and, though the hypothesis possesses those qualities by which the ancient doctrine was suited to the limitations and requirements of the poetical imagination, yet it does not involve that element of fortuitous causation which gave to the ancient doctrine its atheistic character. In the nebular hypothesis the act of creation, though reduced to its simplest form, is still essentially the same as that which a spiritualistic cosmology requires. The first created matter filling the universe is devoid only of outward and developed forms, but contains created within it the forces which shall determine every change and circumstance of its subsequent history. Being thus at once simple and theistic, it appeals to imagination and feeling as a doctrine which at least ought to be true.

Such considerations as these doubtless determined the fate of still another ancient cosmological doctrine, which, though adopted by Aristotle, was regarded with little favor by ancient philosophers generally. For there could be but little support, either from poetry or religion, to the doctrine which denied creation, and held that the order of nature is not, in its cosmical relations, a progression toward an end, or a development, but is rather an endless succession of changes, simple and constant in their elements though infinite in their combinations, which constitute an order without beginning and without termination.

While this latter doctrine was not necessarily materialistic, like that which has been so termed and which was more generally received among the ancients, and though it has the greater scientific simplicity, yet it fails on a point of prime importance, so far as its general credibility is concerned, in that it ignores the main interest which belongs to the problem. Cosmological speculations are properly concerned with the mode or order of the creation, and not with the fact of the creation itself. That the first cosmogonies were written in verse shows the interest almost dramatic which their themes were fitted to inspire. "In the beginning" has never ceased to charm the imagination; and these are almost the only words in our own sacred cosmogony to which the modern geologist has not been compelled to give some ingenious interpretation. That there was a beginning of the order of natural events and successions may be said to be the almost universal faith of Christendom.

The nebular hypothesis, conforming to such preconceptions and to the greatest poetic simplicity, passed the ordeal of unscientific criticism with remarkable success. Not less was its success under a general scientific review. A large number of facts and relations, otherwise unaccountable, follow as at least very probable consequences of its assumptions; and these assumptions were not, at first, without that independent probability which a true scientific theory requires. The existence of the so-called nebulous matter was rendered very probable by the earlier revelations of the telescope; and, though subsequent researches in stellar astronomy have rather diminished than increased the antecedent probability of the theory by successively resolving the nebulae into clusters of star-like constituents—suggesting that all nebulosity may arise from deficiency in the optical powers of the astronomer rather than inhere in the constitution of the nebulae themselves—and thereby invalidating the scientific completeness of the theory, yet the plausible explanations which it still affords of the constitution of the solar system have saved it from condemnation with a considerable number of ingenious thinkers. With astronomers generally, however, it has gradually fallen in esteem. It retains too much of its original character of a happy guess, and has received too little confirmation of a precise and definite kind, to entitle it to rank highly as a physical theory.

But there are two principal grounds on which it will doubtless retain its claim to credibility till its place is supplied, if this ever happens, by some more satisfactory account of cosmical phenomena. To one of these grounds we have just alluded. The details of the constitution of the solar system present, as we have said, many features which suggest a physical origin, directing inquiry as to how they were produced rather than as to why they exist—an inquiry into physical rather than final causes; features of the same mixed character of regularity and apparent accident which are seen in the details of geological or biological phenomena; features not sufficiently regular to indicate a simple primary law, either physical or teleological, nor yet sufficiently irregular to show an absence of law and relation in their production.

The approximation of the orbits of the planets to a common plane, the common direction of their motions around the sun, the approximation of the planes and the directions of their rotations to the planes of their orbits and the directions of their revolutions, the approximatively regular distribution of their distances from the sun, the relations of their satellites to the general features of the primary system—these are some of the facts requiring explanations of the kind which a geologist or a naturalist would give of the distribution of minerals, or stratifications in the crust of the earth, or the distribution of plants and animals upon its surface, phenomena indicating complex antecedent conditions in which the evidence of law is more or less distinct. The absence of that perfection in the solar system, that unblemished completeness, which the ancient astronomy assumed and taught, and the presence, at the same time, of an apparently imperfect regularity, compel us to regard the constitution of the solar system as a secondary and derived product of complicated operations, instead of an archetypal and pure creation.

Such is one of the grounds on which the nebular hypothesis rests. The other is of a more general character. The antecedent probability which the theory lacks, from its inability to prove by independent evidence the fundamental assumption of a nebulous matter, is partially supplied by a still more general hypothesis, to which this theory may be regarded as in some sort a corollary. We refer to the "development hypothesis," or "theory of evolution," a generalization from certain biological phenomena which has latterly attracted great attention from speculative naturalists. This hypothesis has been less fortunate in its history than that of the astronomical one. Inveterate prejudices, insoluble associations of ideas, a want of preparation in the habits of the imagination, were the unscientific obstacles to a general and ready acceptance of this hypothesis at its first promulgation. Though in one of its applications it is identical with the nebular hypothesis, yet, in more direct application to the phenomena of the general life on the earth's surface, it appears so improbable that it has hitherto failed to gain the favor which the nebular hypothesis enjoys. Nevertheless, as a general conception, and independently of its specific use in scientific theories, it has much to recommend it to the speculative mind. It is, as it were, an abstract statement of the order which the intellect expects to find in the phenomena of nature. "Evolution," or the progress "from the homogeneous to the heterogeneous, and from the simple to the complex," is the order of the progress of knowledge itself, and is therefore, naturally enough, sought for as the order in time of all natural phenomena. The specific natural phenomena in which the law of "evolution" is determined by observation as a real and established law are the phenomena of the growth of the individual organism, animal or plant. As a law of psychological phenomena, and even of certain elements of social and historical phenomena, it is also well established. Its extension to the phenomena of the life of the races of organized beings, and to the successions of life on the surface of the earth, is still a speculative conclusion, with about the same degree of scientific probability that the nebular hypothesis possesses. And lastly, in the form of the nebular hypothesis itself, it is extended so as to include the whole series of the phenomena of the universe, and is thus in generality, if accepted as a law of nature, superior to any other generalization in the history of philosophy.

As included in this grander generalization, the nebular hypothesis receives a very important accession of probability, provided that this generalization can be regarded as otherwise well founded. As a part of the induction by which this generalization must be established, if it be capable of proof, the nebular hypothesis acquires a new and important interest.

We are far from being convinced, however, that further inquiry will succeed in establishing so interesting a conclusion. We strongly suspect that the law of "evolution" will fail to appear in phenomena not connected, either directly or remotely, with the life of the individual organism, of the growth of which this law is an abstract description. And, heterodox though the opinion be, we are inclined to accept as the soundest and most catholic assumption, on grounds of scientific method, the too little regarded doctrine of Aristotle, which banishes cosmology from the realm of scientific inquiry, reducing natural phenomena in their cosmical relations to an infinite variety of manifestations (without a discoverable tendency on the whole) of causes and laws which are simple and constant in their ultimate elements.[6]

In rejecting the essential doctrine of "the theory of evolution" or "the development hypothesis" [in cosmology] we must reserve an important conclusion implied in the doctrine which we think is its strongest point. There are several large classes of facts, apparently ultimate and unaccountable, which still bear the marks of being the consequences of the operations of so-called secondary causes—in other words, have the same general character as phenomena which are known to be the results of mixed and conflicting causes, or exhibit at the same time evidence of law and appearance of accident. That such facts should

[6] The laws or archetypes of nature are properly the laws of invariable or unconditional sequence in natural operations. And it is only with the objective relations of these laws, as constituting the order of nature, that natural science is concerned. Their subjective relations, origin, and essential being belong to the province of transcendental metaphysics and to a philosophy of faith. According to this division, there can never arise any conflict between science and faith; for what the one is competent to declare, the other is incompetent to dispute. Science should be free to determine what the order of nature is, and faith equally free to declare the essential nature of causation or creation.

be regarded as evidence of natural operations still unknown, and perhaps unsuspected, is, we think, a legitimate conclusion, and one which is presupposed in "the theory of evolution" and in the nebular hypothesis, but does not necessitate the characteristic assumptions of these speculations. An extension of the sphere of secondary causes, even to the explanation of all the forms of the universe as it now exists, or of all the forms which we may conceive ever to have existed, is a very different thing from adopting the cosmological doctrine of the "development theory." Naturalists who have recently become convinced of the necessity of extending natural explanations to facts in biology hitherto regarded as ultimate and inexplicable, but who are unwilling to adopt the cosmological view implied in the "development theory," have adopted a new name to designate their views. "The derivative theory," or "derivative hypothesis," implies only continuity, not growth or progress, in the succession of races on the surface of the earth. Progress may have been made, as a matter of fact, and the evidence of it may be very conclusive in the geological record; but the fact may still be of secondary importance in the cosmological relations of the phenomena, and the theory ought not, therefore, to give the fact too prominent a place in its nomenclature.

That the constitution of the solar system is not archetypal, as the ancients supposed, but the same corrupt mixture of law and apparent accident that the phenomena of the earth's surface exhibit, is evidence enough that this system is a natural product; [7] and the nebular hypothesis, so far as it is concerned

[7] This argument for physical causes is apparently the reverse of that which Laplace derived from the regularities of the solar system and the theory of probabilities; but in reality the objects of the two arguments are distinct. For the legitimate conclusion from Laplace's computation is, not that the solar system is simply a physical product, but that the causes of its production could not have been irregular. The result of this computation was a probability of two hundred thousand billions to one that the regularities of the solar system are not the effects of chance or irregular causes.

The gist of this argument is to prove simplicity in the antecedents of the solar system; and, had the proportion been still greater, or infinity to one, the argument might have proved a primitive or archetypal character in the with the explanation simply of the production of this system, and independently of its cosmological import, may be regarded as a legitimate theory, even on the ground we have assumed, though on this ground the most probable hypothesis would assimilate the causes which produced the solar system more nearly to the character of ordinary natural operations than the nebular hypothesis does. With a view to such assimilation, and in opposition to "the theory of evolution" as a generalization from the phenomena of growth, we will now propose another generalization, which we cannot but regard as better founded in the laws of nature. We may call it the principle of *counter-movements*—a principle in accordance with which there is no action in nature to which there is not some counteraction, and no production in nature by which in infinite ages there can result an infinite product. In biological phenomena this principle is familiarly illustrated by the counterplay of the forces of life and death, of nutrition and waste, of growth and degeneration, and of similar opposite effects. In geology the movements of the materials of the earth's crust through the counteractions of the forces by which the strata are elevated and denuded, depressed and deposited, ground to mud or hardened to rock, are all of the compensative sort; and the movements of the gaseous and liquid oceans which surround the earth manifest still more markedly the principle of countermovements in the familiar phenomena of the weather.

Of what we may call cosmical weather, in the interstellar spaces, little is known. Of the general cosmical effects of the opposing actions of heat and gravitation, the great dispersive

---

movements of this system. It is therefore in the limitations, and not in the magnitude, of this proportion that there is any tendency to show physical antecedence. Hence it is not from the regularities of the solar system, but from its complexity, that its physical origin is justly inferred.

Regarding the *law of causation* as universal, since, if not implied in the very search for causes, it is at least the broadest and the best established induction from natural phenomena, we conclude that the appearance of accident among the manifestations of law is proof of the existence of complex antecedent conditions and of physical causation, and that the absence of this appearance is proof of simple and primitive law.

and concentrative principles of the universe, we can at present only form vague conjectures; but that these two principles are the agents of vast countermovements in the formation and destruction of systems of worlds, always operative in never-ending cycles and in infinite time, seems to us to be by far the most rational supposition which we can form concerning the matter. And indeed, in one form or another, the agencies of heat and gravitation must furnish the explanations of the circumstances and the peculiarities of solar and sidereal systems. These are the agents which the nebular hypothesis supposes; but by this hypothesis they are supposed to act under conditions opposed to that general analogy of natural operations expressed by the law of countermovements. Their relative actions are regarded as directed, under certain conditions, toward a certain definite result; and this being attained, their formative agency is supposed to cease, the system to be finished, and the creation, though a continuous process, to be a limited one.

It should be noticed, however, in favor of the nebular hypothesis, that its assumptions are made, not arbitrarily, in opposition to the general analogy of natural operations, but because they furnish at once and very simply certain mechanical conditions from which systems analogous to the solar system may be shown to be derivable. The dispersive agency of heat is supposed to furnish the primordial conditions upon which, as the heat is gradually lost from the clouds of nebulous matter, the agency of gravitation produces the condensations, the motions, and the disruptions of the masses which subsequently become suns and planets and satellites. And if the mechanical conditions assumed in this hypothesis could be shown to be the only ones by which similar effects could be produced, the hypothesis would, without doubt, acquire a degree of probability amounting almost to certainty, even in spite of the absence of independent proof that matter has ever existed in the nebulous form.

But the mechanical conditions of the problem have never been determined in this exhaustive manner, nor are the conditions assumed in the nebular hypothesis able to determine any other than the general circumstances of the solar system, such as it is supposed to have in common with similar systems among the stars. A more detailed deduction would probably require as many separate, arbitrary, and additional hypotheses as there are special circumstances to be accounted for. Until, therefore, it can be shown that the nebular hypothesis is the only one which can account mechanically for the agency of heat and gravitation in the formation of special systems of worlds, like the solar system, its special cosmological and mechanical features ought to be regarded with suspicion, as opposed to the general analogy of natural operations. . . .

V

JOHN STUART MILL
A COMMEMORATIVE NOTICE [1]

The name of John Stuart Mill [2] is so intimately associated with most of the principal topics of modern philosophical discussion and with the gravest of open questions, with so many of the weightiest subjects of unsettled theory and practice, that it would be difficult to say for which of his many works his fame is at present the greatest or is most likely to endure. Those subjects in the treatment of which the originality of his position was the least were those in which the qualities most characteristic of him, and for which his writings have been most esteemed, appear in clearest light. Unlike most other great thinkers and masters of dialectics, he did not seek to display what his own invention had contributed to the arguments, or his observation to the premises, in his discussion of philosophical and practical questions. On the contrary, he seemed to be indifferent to the appearance and reputation of originality, and actuated by a singleness of purpose and a loyalty to the views of his teachers in philosophy and science which were inconsistent with motives of personal vanity. The exercise of his admirably trained dialectical powers doubtless afforded him intrinsic delight, the joy of play, or of spontaneity of power; but it was none the less always subordinated to moral purposes which were clearly defined in his youth and loyally pursued through an active intellectual life for nearly half a century. But his broad practical aims were

1 [From the *Proceedings of the American Academy of Arts and Sciences*, 1873-74.]

2 [John Stuart Mill (1806-1873), English philosopher and economist. His main philosophical works, and the ones which most influenced Wright, were *System of Logic*, 9th edition (1875); *Utilitarianism* (1863); *Examination of Sir W. Hamilton's Philosophy* (1865); and *Three Essays on Religion* (1874). Cf. Chapter 10 of *Theories of Scientific Method from the Renaissance to the Nineteenth Century*, R. W. Blake, C. J. Ducasse, and E. H. Madden.]

never allowed, on the other hand, to pervert the integrity and honesty of his intellect. Though an advocate all his life, urging reasons for unpopular measures of reform, and defenses of an unpopular philosophy or criticisms of the prevailing one, he was not led, as advocates too frequently are, to the indiscriminate invention and use of bad and good arguments. He weighed his arguments as dispassionately as if his aim had been pure science. Rarely have strength of emotion and purpose and strength of intellect been combined in a thinker with such balance and harmony. The strength of his moral emotions gave him insights or premises which had been overlooked by the previous thinkers whose views he expounded or defended. This advantage over his predecessors was conspicuous in the form he gave to the utilitarian theory of moral principles, and in what was strictly original in his *Principles of Political Economy.*

In the latter, the two chief points of originality were, first, his treatment of the subject as a matter of pure abstract science, like geometry; or as an account of the means which are requisite to attain given ends in economics, or the cost needed to procure a given value, without bringing into the discussion the irrelevant practical questions, whether this cost should be incurred or whether the end were on the whole desirable. These questions really belong to other branches of practical philosophy—to the sciences of legislation, politics, and morals, to which the principles of political economy stand in the relation of an abstract science to sciences of applied principles and concrete matters. But, secondly, while thus limiting the province of this science, he introduced into it premises from the moral nature of man, by the omission of which previous writers had been led to conclusions in the science of a character gloomy and forbidding. The theory of population of Malthus,[3] as elaborated by Ricardo,[4]

3 [Thomas Robert Malthus (1766-1834), English economist. His principal book, *Essay on the Principle of Population* (1798), contains the famous "Malthusian theory": since there will always be more people in the world than can be fed, wars and disease are necessary to kill off the extra population.]

4 [David Ricardo (1772-1823), English economist, published his important *Principles of Political Economy and Taxation* in 1817. Wright apparently

seemed to subject the human race to a hopeless necessity of poverty in the masses. Whether the principle of population did really necessitate this conclusion would depend, Mill taught, on more than the capacity of a soil to support a *maximum* population with the least subsistence needed for the labor of production. The principle applies without qualification to the animal world in general and to savage men; but not to progressive communities of men, in which foresight and prudence, with moral and social aspirations, are forces of more or less influence in checking increase in population, and in improving the condition of the masses. The poorest, the most wretched, are not in the same condition of want in all communities of men. The poorest savage is objectively in a worse condition than the poorest civilized man.

Mill did not oppose the views of his predecessors nor their manner of treatment, as so many other writers had done: he carried out their mode of regarding the science as a physical one, but with a thoroughness which brought to light considerations materially modifying their conclusions. The prospects of mankind are not hopeless so long as men are capable of aspirations, foresight, and hope, though they may be gloomy enough in view of the slow working of these forces. What these forces have to oppose, however, is not the resistance of an immovable necessity, but only the force of inveterate customs. To the sentimental objection that the laws of political economy are cruel, and therefore not true, Mill humorously replied that he knew of no law more cruel than that of gravity, which would put us all to death were we not always vigilantly on our guard against it.

With a full, perhaps a too extreme appreciation of moral forces as elements in the problems of political economy, Mill still treated the science as an abstract one—as a science of conditional propositions, a science applicable to the practical

---

refers to Ricardo's "iron law of wages," according to which an organization can be successful in the long run only by paying workers a minimum living wage.]

problems of morals and politics but not in itself treating of them. For example, wars are expensive, and the establishment of a new industry is also an expense which the principles of political economy can estimate; but it does so without deciding whether war or an industry ought under given circumstances to be undertaken.

Moral forces are real agents affecting the future of the human race. As causes of effects, they are calculable forces, and as means to ends are proper subjects of the abstract science of political economy. It was because Mr. Mill believed in "moral causation" (the name he gave to what had indiscriminately been called the doctrine of *necessity* in human volition), and because he himself was powerfully and predominantly actuated throughout his life by high moral considerations, that he gave such emphasis to the moral elements in political economy, and made room for hope—for a sober, rational hope—respecting the practical conclusions and applications of the science; seeing that hope can subsist with the desire that inspires it, provided the desire is instrumental in effecting what is hoped for. It was because he believed in "moral causation" that he treated political science, in general, in the manner and by the methods of physical philosophy, or as a science of causes and effects. He believed that he himself and his generation would effect much for the future of mankind. His faith was that we live in times in which broad principles of justice, persistently proclaimed, end in carrying the world with them.

His hopefulness, generosity, and courage, and a chivalric, almost romantic disposition in him, seemed to those least acquainted with him inconsistent with the utilitarian philosophy of morals, which he not only professed, but earnestly and even zealously maintained. The "greatest happiness principle" was with him a religious principle, to which every impulse in his nature, high or low, was subordinated. It was for him not only a *test* of rational rules of conduct (which is all that could be, or was, claimed for it in his philosophy of morals), but it became for him a leading motive and sanction of conduct in his theory of life. That other minds differently constituted would be most effectively influenced to the nobility of right conduct by other sanctions and motives, to which the utilitarian principle ought to be regarded as only a remote philosophical test or rational standard, was what he believed and taught. Unlike Bentham, his master in practical philosophy, he felt no contempt for the claims of sentiment and made no intolerant demand for toleration. He sincerely welcomed intelligent and earnest opposition with a deference due to truth itself and to a just regard for the diversities in men's minds from differences of education and natural dispositions. These diversities even appeared to him essential to the completeness of the examination which the evidences of truth demand. Opinions positively erroneous, if intelligent and honest, are not without their value, since the progress of truth is a succession of mistakes and corrections. Truth itself, unassailed by erroneous opinion, would soon degenerate into narrowness and error. The errors incident to individuality of mind and character are means, in the attrition of discussion, of keeping the truth bright and untarnished, and even of bringing its purity to light. The human mind cannot afford to forget its past aberrations. These, as well as its true discoveries, are indispensable guides; nor can it ever afford to begin from the starting point in its search for truth, in accordance with the too confident method of more ambitious philosophers.

Such being his loyalty and generosity, it is not surprising that Mill obtained a much wider acceptance of utilitarian doctrines, and a more intelligent recognition of their real import, than previous thinkers of his school had secured. He redeemed the word "utility" from the ill repute into which it had fallen, and connected noble conceptions and motives with its philosophical meaning. It is now no longer a synonym of the ignoble or base, or the name of that quality in conduct, or in anything which conduces to the satisfaction of desires common to all men. He made it mean clearly the quality in human customs and rules of conduct which conduces to realize conditions and dispositions which for men (though not for swine) are practicable and are the most desirable, their desirableness being tested by the actual preference which those who possess them have for them as elements in their own happiness. This meaning of utility includes the highest motives in whose satisfaction an individual's happiness can consist, and not the baser ones alone; not even the base ones at all, so far as they obstruct the sources of a greater happiness than they can afford. It is now no longer a paradox to the intelligent student of Mill's philosophy that he should prefer, as he has avowed, the worst evil which could be inflicted on him against his will to the pains of a voluntary sophistication of his intellect in respect to the more serious concerns of life. . . .

In politics he belonged to what is called the school of "philosophical radicals," who are, as he defined them, those who in politics follow the common manner of philosophers, who trust neither to tradition nor to intuition for the warrant of political rights and duties but base the right to power in the state on the ability to govern wisely and justly, and, seeing their country badly governed, seek for the cause of this evil and for means to remedy it. This cause they found to be in "the Aristocratical Principle," since, in the present imperfect condition of human nature, no governing class would attend to those interests of the many which were in conflict with their own, or could be expected to give to any interests not their own any but a secondary consideration. The remedy for this evil they found in a modified democratic principle, namely, the better ability and disposition of the many to look after their own interests than any dominant few could have or would be likely to have—provided the many, or their representatives, are enlightened enough to know their true interests and how to serve them. The motto of this radicalism was "Enmity to the Aristocratical Principle." From this creed sprung Mill's ardent hostility toward the South in their rebellion against our national government, and his hearty espousal of extreme antislavery views.

But a democracy may be tyrannical toward minorities, and, if unchecked, is likely to become so; and, what is worse, is likely to become an unprincipled tyrant, less influenced by considerations of justice or prudence than a governing class would be.

This fear made Mill distrust extreme forms of democracy and government by mere majorities. Accordingly, among his later works, his *Considerations on Representative Government* undertakes to devise checks to the abuse of power by majorities. But it is evident that Mill's greatest trust was in those influences which have given to communities the ability, and thence the power and right, to govern themselves—namely, their intelligence and moral integrity, or that which reduces the necessity of government by force to the fewest functions and occasions. His famous *Essay on Liberty* sought to establish, on grounds of moral principle, restraints of governmental force, in whatever way it might be exercised, whether in the form of public law or of public opinion; neither of which in any form of government is likely to be wiser beyond its proper sphere of duty than those it seeks to control. Government in advanced communities, capable of self-government, should not be of the parental type or degree of power. Coercion, which in itself is an evil, becomes a wrong where persuasion, rational discussion, and conviction are capable of effecting the same ends, especially when these ends are less urgent than the need of security and self-protection in a community, for which it is the proper duty of government by force to provide. To place government in the hands of those sufficiently intelligent, whose true interests are most affected by it, and to limit its province and its functions as much as possible, leaving as much as possible to noncoercive agencies, was the simple abstract creed of Mill's political philosophy.

The *Essay on Liberty* and his later essay on *The Subjection of Women* exhibit the ardent, emotional, enthusiastic, perhaps not the soundest, side of Mr. Mill's mental character and observation of human nature. Yet he cannot be said to have been without much experience in the practical art of government. He was in immediate charge of the "political department," so called, of the East India House for more than twenty years. It was during this period, and in the midst of active employments, that his *Logic* and *Political Economy* were written. Both were thought out in the vigor of life and at the summit of his powers.

His mind and pen were never idle. At about the age of fifty, he published selections from his occasional short writings for reviews. These had more than a passing interest, since in them, as in all his writings, great and often new principles of criticism are lucidly set forth. In all his writings, his judgments are valued by his readers, not as judgments on occasional matters by a current or conventional standard, but as tests and illustrations of new standards of criticism which have a general and enduring interest, especially to the examining minds of youth.

With a tact almost feminine, Mill avoided open war on abstract grounds. The principles of his philosophy were set forth in their applications, and were advocated by bringing them down in application to the common sense or instinctive, unanalyzed judgments of his readers. His conclusions in psychology and on the fundamental principles of philosophy were nowhere systematically set forth. In his *Logic,* they were rather assumed, and made the setting of his views of the science, than defended on general grounds; though, from his criticisms of adverse views on the principles of logic, it was sufficiently apparent what his philosophy and psychological doctrines were.

English-speaking and -reading people had so completely forgotten, or had so obscurely understood, the arguments of their greatest thinkers that the inroad of German speculation had almost overwhelmed the protest of these thinkers against the a priori philosophy. English-speaking people are not metaphysical, and Mill respected their prejudice. But when the philosophy of Sir William Hamilton,[5] professing to combine the Scottish and German reactions against Hume with what science had demonstrated as the necessary limits of human knowledge, was about to become the prevalent philosophy of England and America, it was not merely an opportunity but almost a necessity for the representative of the greatest English thinkers (himself among the greatest) to re-examine the claims of the

[5] [Sir William Hamilton (1788-1856) was professor of philosophy at the University of Edinburgh. His principal works, *Philosophy of the Unconditioned* (1829) and *Lectures on Metaphysics and Logic* (1858, 1860), influenced Wright greatly. See Appendix I of the present volume.]

a priori philosophy, and either to acknowledge the failure of his own attempt to revive the doctrines of his predecessors, or to refute and overthrow their most powerful British antagonist. Accordingly Mill's *Examination of Sir William Hamilton's Philosophy*, published in 1865, when he was nearly sixty years old but in the full vigor and maturity of his powers, was his greatest effort in polemical writing. That the reputation of Sir William Hamilton as a thinker was greatly diminished by this examination cannot be doubted. Nor can it be doubted that the pendulum of philosophical opinion has begun, through Mill's clear expositions and vigorous defense of the experience philosophy, to move again toward what was a century and a half ago the prevalent English philosophy. That its future movements will be less extreme in either direction, and that the the amplitude of its oscillations have continually diminished in the past through the progress of philosophical discussion, were beliefs with which his studies in philosophy and his generous hopefulness inspired him. Men are still born either Platonists or Aristotelians; but by their education through a more and more free and enlightened discussion, and by progress in the sciences, they are restrained more and more from going to extremes in the directions of their native biases.

In Mill's *Examination of Hamilton,* and in his last great work, the annotated edition of his father's *Analysis of the Phenomena of the Human Mind,* many valuable subsidiary contributions are made to the sciences of logic and psychology. But in all his writings on these subjects his attention was directed to their bearings on the traditional problems and discussions of general philosophy. The modern developments of psychology as a branch of experimental science and in connection with physiology deeply interested him; but they did not engage him in their pursuit, although they promise much toward the solution of unsettled questions. His mental powers were trained for a different though equally important service to science—the service of clear and distinct thought, the understanding, first of all, of that for which closer observation and the aid of experiment are needed: the precise comprehension and pertinent putting of questions. The progress of science has not yet outgrown the need of guidance by the intellectual arts of logic and method which are still equal in importance to those of experiment. The imagination of the scientific inquisitor of nature, the fertility of his invention, his ability to frame hypotheses or put pertinent questions, though still generally dependent on his good sense and his practical training in experimental science, are susceptible still of furtherance and improvement by the abstract studies of logic and method. Open questions on the psychological conditions of vision are to be settled, Mill thought, only when someone so unfortunate as to be born blind is fortunate enough to be born a philosopher.

Mill has been aptly compared to Locke. Their philosophies were fundamentally the same. Both were "philosophical radicals" and political reformers. "What Locke was to the liberal movements of the seventeenth century, Mr. Mill has more than been to the liberal movement of the nineteenth century." He was born on the 20th of May, 1806, and died on the 8th of May, 1873, having nearly reached the age of sixty-seven. Previous to the brief illness from which he died, he retained unimpaired his mental vigor and industry; and though it may not be said that he lived to see the hopes of his youth fully realized, yet his efforts have met with a degree of success in later years which he did not anticipate. His followers are still few both in politics and in philosophy. So far was he from restoring the doctrines of his school as the dominant philosophy of England that, according to his own estimate, "we may still count in England twenty a priori or spiritualist philosophers for every partisan of the doctrine of experience." But it was for the practical applications of this doctrine in politics and in morals, rather than for the theoretical recognition of it in general, that he most earnestly strove; and we should probably find in England and America today a much larger proportion, among those holding meditated and deliberate opinions on practical matters, who are in these the disciples of Mill than can be found among the students of abstract philosophy.

APPENDIX

I. [PORTRAIT OF WRIGHT][1]

by E. W. Gurney

Though we were classmates, I knew Chauncey but slightly in college; our real acquaintance began in the autumn after our graduation, in 1852. Then I lived for a few weeks in Cambridge; and he, Chase, and I fell into the way of spending our evenings together. By some freak of memory, one of these evenings remains still distinct in my mind, although all the others are a blank. I can still see the room—and almost the formulae of Taylor's theorem, over a point in which the talk began—as Chauncey sat discoursing to me till morning upon the metaphysical conceptions underlying the methods of fluxions and the calculus. I mention this only because it illustrates to me how like in mental habit was the young fellow of two-and-twenty to the man of two-and-forty. That evening was the prototype of thousands we afterwards spent together; and had I, twenty years later, raised the same question, the chances are that he would have unconsciously reproduced in all essentials the same thoughts and in the same order. The tenacity, by the way, of Chauncey's hold upon all the results of his past thinking was marvelous, and showed, if I may say so, how organically connected was his whole structure of thought. "You remember," he would say, "the definition I evolved of this—or the law I formulated of that—in such and such a talk with you"—and the conversation, it might be, had occurred five or ten years before. . . .

Cave hominem unius libri, says the proverb; which had probably a more frequent application once, when books were rarer.

[1] [A letter written by E. W. Gurney to J. B. Thayer in 1877. Cf. *Letters*, pp. 361-383. Gurney became professor of history at Harvard College in 1869 and was the first Dean of the College (1869-1876).]

At any rate, Chauncey was the only striking illustration that has come in my way of the immense amount of nutriment that an original and meditative mind may draw from a single author. Sir William Hamilton, at this period of Chauncey's life, held for several years substantially the same place in his intellectual life that was afterwards occupied by Mill and Darwin. You will still remember how refreshing it was to us in our college days to pass from the text of Reid,[2] with his homely, practical way of applying his common sense to metaphysical problems, to the notes furnished by Dr. Walker [3] from Hamilton's edition of Reid, almost obtrusively precise, acute, and learned. It was like turning your eyes from the motions of a sturdy ploughman to those of a trained athlete. The taste then acquired for Hamilton was soon afterwards more fully gratified by the reproduction in this country of nearly all that he had then published, and the College Library copy of Hamilton's edition of Reid supplied the rest. Later, after Hamilton's death, came a fresh interest and new material from the publication of his lectures on Logic and Metaphysics. Though Chauncey, in after years, abandoned all that was peculiar in Hamilton's system, as for instance his explanation of the origin of the so-called necessary truths, I doubt whether any other philosophical author would have aided his development in so many ways. Our friend all through his life, so far back at least as my acquaintance with him runs, was utterly averse to reading. All that he required from books, and all that his nature allowed him to obtain from them, was stimulus and direction to his own thoughts from the questions they raised, and to a less extent from the solutions they offered. Now, Hamilton, from the super-

[2] [Thomas Reid (1710-1796), who succeeded Adam Smith as professor of philosophy at the University of Glasgow, was the founder of the Scottish intuitionist school (cf. Introduction to the present volume). The key to Reid's philosophy is his effort to escape from Hume's skeptical conclusions.]

[3] [James Walker (1794-1874) was a Unitarian clergyman and president of Harvard College from 1853 to 1860. Before his presidency he taught philosophy and Wright was one of his students. Cf. E. H. Madden, "Chauncey Wright's Life and Work: Some New Material," *Journal of the History of Ideas*, Vol. XV (1954), pp. 447 ff.]

abundance of the stores of learning which he brings forth upon all things, great and small, in the history of philosophy, was exactly suited to meet this want of Chauncey, while the easy mastery that he has over his learning and the new setting which he gives to others' thoughts save him from becoming pedantic and tiresome. . . .

Another book which, in his way, he read much at that time was Whewell's *History and Philosophy of the Inductive Sciences.* This gave him such knowledge as he needed for his speculative purposes of the development of science, just as Hamilton incidentally did of the progress of philosophy. Brande's *Cyclopaedia* served him as a ready repository of the scientific or other data he might happen to need in his meditations. I remember, too, his being interested in List's [4] *Political Economy* in those early days, and the ingenious manner in which he used, then, to defend the theory of protection to domestic industry.

In the spring of 1857 I went to Cambridge to live, and from that time, as you know, was on terms of the greatest intimacy with Chauncey. Not very long after my migration, he moved from his old quarters in Bow Street to Little's Block, in which my rooms were; and, for eight or ten years, there were few days in which we did not spend several hours together. It was about this time, I think, that he began to teach philosophy in Professor Agassiz's School; and the pleasure he took in this occupation for several winters was very great. It gave him a fresh motive for going systematically through Hamilton, with whom he was already so familiar; and it furnished him with the audience which alone was needed to make Chauncey's happiness in following out his trains of thought complete. Not very far from this time I should place the earliest of Chauncey's review articles that I definitely remember, based on Blodget's [5] *Meteor-*

[4] [Friedrich List (1789-1846), German economist. List's "Political Economy," to which Gurney refers, is *Outlines of American Political Economy* (1827).]

[5] [Lorin Blodget (1823-1901) was an American statistician and climatologist who did his major work at the Smithsonian Institute.]

ology of the United States. These, too, were the days of the *Septem,* the little knot of men who passed so many pleasant evenings together in Little's Block but whose motto, in the pentameter verse of one of their number, has something tragic in it, when I think of the one dark thread in our friend's life—*quod placet his fas est, quod placet hi faciunt.* How much Chauncey enjoyed those evenings and that society!

It must have been in 1859 or 1860 that Chauncey first felt the influence which was to be more powerful than any other in giving direction and color to his intellectual life. This was the publication of Darwin's *Origin of Species.* We read it and re-read it aloud together, and talked over it and the reviews that appeared of it interminably. The ground had been prepared for the seed by Chauncey's interest in theoretic geology, and the argument for the sufficiency of causes now in operation to explain past changes in the condition of the earth; by the discussions which had gone on for years in Cambridge between Agassiz [6] and Gray [7] concerning the true nature of the terms "genus" and "species"; and by the fruitfulness, already shown, of the historical method in dealing with social phenomena. I think I am not mistaken in putting the publication of Maine's [8] *Ancient Law*—my interest in which was shared by Chauncey—very near that of the *Origin of Species.*

Up to this time, however, the abstract theory of evolution had not found favor in Chauncey's mind. In illustration of this, I

6 [Jean Louis Rodolphe Agassiz (1807-1873), Swiss-U.S. naturalist, geologist, and, beginning in 1848, teacher at Harvard University, was a strong opponent of Darwin's notion of the mutability of species.]

7 [Asa Gray (1810-1888), American botanist and Harvard professor, was a sympathetic exponent of Darwinian principles. In addition to great scientific contributions to the Darwinian controversy, he made important contributions to the *logic* of Darwinian theory—showing, e.g., that the concept of natural selection need not be understood as eliminating the theological argument from design.]

8 [Sir Henry J. S. Maine (1822-1888), English comparative jurist and historian, published *Ancient Law* in 1861; Darwin published the *Origin of Species* in 1859. Maine wanted to indicate some of the earliest ideas of mankind, as they are reflected in ancient law, and to point out the relation of these ideas to modern thought.]

recall, years previously, a talk with him about the *Vestiges of Creation,* into which, I think, he had barely dipped, and how lightly he regarded the thesis itself, as well as the arguments. I remember, too, how decided were his leanings for Cuvier[9] as against Geoffroy St.-Hilaire, and how destitute of attraction for him had been the nebular hypothesis. To his mind, no theory of evolution would have commended itself on a priori grounds; but the cumulative argument, based on observation and experiment, of the *Origin of Species,* in harmony as it was with his own habits of thought, carried with it complete conviction. A real explanation, so far as it went, had been furnished as to the manner in which the organic world had come to take its present form; and, more and more, as time went on, it became the predominant intellectual interest of his life to study the problems, physical and metaphysical, which the acceptance of this explanation presented.

Not only was the direct influence of Darwin on Chauncey's scientific views thus great, but hardly less curious and important was the reflex influence upon his purely speculative opinions of the questions in which he was now most interested and the methods employed in their solution. There was no sudden change; for Chauncey's opinions had been too well considered and were too organically connected to admit of any serious modification, except that which comes from a changed attitude of the mind as a whole. Such philosophical conversion, in a serious, powerful thinker like Chauncey, proceeds so gradually that one who is in constant intercourse with him is almost as unconscious of the process as of the imperceptible changes that come with time in the expression of a face. As I look back on those years, however, I can see that Hamilton was less and less resorted to, except for his learning and on points of which the treatment is not affected by fundamental philosophical conceptions, and that Bain and Mill came to furnish the topics of

9 [Cuvier, (Georges) Léopold Chrétien Frédéric Dagobert, Baron (1769-1832), French naturalist, claimed that every species was explicitly created for its own special purpose and every organ for one specific function. With this view he directly opposed Geoffroy Saint-Hilaire.]

his thought. I put them in this order because I think it the chronological one of his intimacy with them. The interest in the inductive and semiphysiological treatment of the old psychological problems which led so unpracticed a reader through Bain's two thick octavos, ponderous in every sense, was an indication of whither he was drifting in his philosophy. I remember that Professor Winlock [10] was laid up for several weeks by lameness at about this time, and how great satisfaction Chauncey had in inducing him to read Bain, and in discussing with so acute a man Bain's statements and solutions. Bain, however, was a specialist, and not a philosopher; and, after his facts had been fairly taken up by Chauncey's mind, his volumes went upon the shelf as books merely of reference. It was Mill who succeeded Hamilton as Chauncey's constant, cherished philosophical companion; and the tie grew stronger and stronger to the end of Chauncey's life. . . .

I have dwelt at this length upon the development of Chauncey's philosophical opinions because he was in a sense peculiar to himself among all the men I have known, "a being breathing thoughtful breath"; and because I believe that I am the only friend who was continuously intimate with him during the whole period of their development, and also sufficiently interested in such questions to lead him to discourse upon them freely. During the last half-dozen years of his life, after my marriage, I saw him, to be sure, less constantly; but, happily for me, he always kept up his habit of reading to me what he had been writing, and of talking over the philosophical problems that were interesting him. I was thus kept fairly well acquainted with the thread of his speculations to the end.

Let me try now, however imperfectly, to give form and proportion to my impressions of Chauncey's character and mind. One so seldom attempts to bring to a focus the myriad impressions which lurk in the memory that the best image one can

[10] [Joseph Winlock (1826-1875), American astronomer and mathematician, became director of the Harvard College Observatory in 1866. His interests were especially in the astronomy of position but he also championed some of the earliest spectroscopic studies of stars and nebulae.]

hope to bring out will seem very rude to those who were familiar with the original.

One would naturally begin with the physique—so sound, so massive, so inert, and yet capable of so much effort and endurance! His body was like an engine that, if sufficiently stoked with sleep and food, however irregular the intervals, was always in condition to do what was required of it. Heavy as were the draughts he made at times on the reserves of his constitution, the springs of its strength long seemed unfailing. Save one ugly attack [in 1863], I can recall no ailment of his, great or small, during the many years of our daily intercourse. Especially notable was his exemption from all nervous discomforts, like headache. His sleep was profound beyond that of childhood. He always kept excessively late hours, but slept steadily from seven to nine hours, be his hour of going to bed what it might. He formed these habits in the days when, at Mrs. Lyman's, Mary Walker was ready and glad to give him his breakfast at whatever hour he presented himself; and, with characteristic phlegm, he adhered for life, without regard to the obstacles that boardinghouse keepers or friends might throw in his way, to a disposition of his hours that suited him. So deep was his sleep that you could pull him out of bed in the morning without fairly rousing him. For the first hour or two after he got up, he seemed to feel an owl-like strangeness in the bright world about him; and it was only by degrees that he recovered full possession of his faculties. He dreamed little; and his only recurring form of dream was that of flying, or rather floating in the air, a little distance above the ground. After the complete repose of these nights, by about twelve or one o'clock in the day, he began life again perfectly fresh, no matter how late his hours had been, nor for how long a time late hours had been kept. The sluggishness that accompanied the soundness of Chauncey's body extended to his senses, with the exception of that of sight. This was marvelously keen, as well as alert; the others were content to respond when called upon. Given a sound body, a sluggish temperament, and a mind always occupied on some purely intellectual problem, one might, I fancy, anticipate the chief features of Chauncey's character, if one failed to do justice to its finer qualities. Calm, gentle, unassuming; ready to be pleased; demanding little of his friends; as pure as a woman in thought and speech; fond of children, and unwearied in giving them pleasure; free from passion to a defect; never selfish, though at times, from preoccupation of mind or from lack of imagination, not wholly considerate; deficient in ambition; devoid of jealousy and envy; perfectly honorable and perfectly amiable—there stand out in the memory of his oldest friends, as the last impressions of his character, the same large features, great simplicity and great dignity, which would have struck an observer meeting him for the first time.

One is impressed, in going through life, with the disparity among men in the use that is made of their Christian names. Some seem to lose them in childhood, and outside of their own families are known only by the family name, with or without a prefix, according to the degree of intimacy. At the other extreme stand those who have in truth a "given" name, and with whom men slip easily and unconsciously into the use of it. One seldom sees so notable an illustration of this gift for creating easy relations as in our friend. When one considers how formidable to most men such an intelligence as his in itself would be, it speaks volumes for his simplicity, sweetness, and modesty of character that he should have been known as "Chauncey" by all who came much in contact with him.

Of this intelligence, which made Chauncey so marked a man, let me end this long letter by trying to give you my impressions with a little more method than came naturally in speaking of his philosophical development. Marvelous as that intelligence was—quite unmatched, indeed, within its own great range, in my experience of men—its limitations were very sharply marked.

Chauncey's intellect was very little fed through his emotions; and to the beauties of nature, of art, and of literature, his susceptibilities were neither quick nor cultivated—striking and novel as were his comments at times on such matters, from acuteness of observation or force of intellect. With little relish for literature as literature, with little call for any class of facts that would demand much reading or resort to foreign tongues, whatever aptitudes he possessed for acquiring languages remained entirely dormant. History, except as occasionally a fact caught in conversation or chance reading might furnish him a peg on which to fasten some thread of political or social speculation, had little interest for him.

On the other hand, no fact concerning the mind itself or the material universe came amiss to him. Each at once fell into its proper place, determined by its relations to other facts already known; and, thanks to this web of natural association, it was seldom that what he had once acquired slipped out of his memory past recall. Hence, although he was no reader, as I have said, and not a student in the ordinary sense of that term, the amount of his knowledge was prodigious. The workings of Chauncey's mind might well have suggested to Plato his doctrine of reminiscence; for one could easily fancy that the universe and its laws had been once mirrored in his mind in their completeness, and that experience and meditation were simply bringing out into consciousness the dim lines of the image they had left. The acquisitions of several men whom I have known have excited my admiration; but in the case of no one but Chauncey have they caused wonder. However vast the other structures, one knew the process by which they had been reared, and could reckon, if I may say so, the number of days' work which had gone into them; but of Chauncey's knowledge one could only say, *crescit occulto velut arbor aevo.* . . . You who knew Chauncey in his boyhood, when the foundation of his scientific acquisitions were laid by your excellent teacher at Northampton of whom he has often spoken to me, can doubtless recall the beginnings of his scientific knowledge; but when I became intimate with him, at twenty-five, his easy mastery of the principles of all the physical sciences and of psychology, the only subjects about which he ever much occupied himself, made his knowledge then seem as complete and round as it was fifteen years later. The increase that came with time seemed, even to one in constant intercourse with him, rather a process of development and expansion than, as in the case of most men, one of accretion. He worked in no laboratory; neither botany nor geology drew him into the field; when he took up a book, it was only on a subject that interested him, and it was usually simply to look over the table of contents, and to read a page here and a page there to give him what was characteristic in the author's treatment of his theme; yet so thoroughly did he possess his subjects in their principles, so fully had he worked them out in his meditations, that, the place for every new fact being always ready, the new fact was sure to reach him as if through the air. Though a specialist in no scientific subject—for he early gave up all continuous study of mathematics—few specialists could have failed to find an hour's talk with him fruitful in furthering their investigations.

When scientific acquisitions so great had been made, as it were, by the way, without resort to the apparatus of books or instruments with which men commonly lay siege to their subjects, without the usual persistent application of months or years to the mastery of one, the question could not but arise in the mind of a friend of Chauncey, What distinction might not this man achieve, if, enamored of a science or stimulated by ambition, he should concentrate his powers within a narrower field? The better one knew Chauncey, however, the more clearly one saw how completely so exceptional a mind carried the laws of its workings within itself. His temperament was too sluggish, his interest in discoveries too purely philosophical, to allow him to make his mark as an investigator, in spite of the subtilty and fertility of his mind in devising experiments when he desired to satisfy himself upon a doubtful point. For continuous work in the field of theoretical physics, for which his mathematical ability and his large scientific imagination seemed especially to fit him, I do not remember that he ever showed any inclination. Work of this kind would have involved an amount of drudgery to which Chauncey would have hardly subjected himself, except from a keen interest in solving a particular problem. He showed his power to cope with such problems when they came in his way, but he did not seek them for their own sake. In a word, Chauncey's mind did not work under the discipline of the will. It was not indolent: few brains indeed worked more incessantly; but it always shrunk from uncongenial work, and all effort with him that was not spontaneous was uncongenial.

Few powerful minds had less of the artistic element, in the ordinary sense of that term, than his; yet the character of the satisfaction he found in making his mind a mirror of the intelligible world—the world of law without him and within—is best illustrated, I think, by the delight that the eye sensitive to material beauty finds in gazing at a lovely prospect or noble work of art, and the mind in analyzing the charm. He lived, indeed, in an intellectual paradise in which all his powers found full activity and were free from all constraint; nor was the friendly ear, which was his one need more, often lacking into which to pour the results of each day's meditations. Was it a paradise, or was it rather a Circe's garden, which sapped a feeble will, and beguiled him from the tasks that might have opened up some unexplored corner of the universe, or have given mankind a Wright's law, and himself a name? I cling to the paradise theory; but I may be biased by the consciousness of all that I have enjoyed and gained from the manner of life he led. Some of the external conditions of his life one would have wished changed, notably his mode of breadwinning. The computations which, for many years, he made for the Nautical Almanac—as not demanding from him more than two or three hours' work a day, and making no draughts on his thinking power—furnished in one sense an occupation as favorable as could be imagined for a mind that desired simply leisure for speculation; but, unfortunately, the temptation to him was irresistible to crowd the work into the last two or three months of the year within which it was to be finished, and to try to reduce himself during this period to the insensibility of a computing machine, working from noon until two or three o'clock in the morning. For a time, the prospect of perfect independence for nine or ten months sufficed to carry him through this yearly period of purgatory; but, in the course of years, he found stronger stimulants necessary to support him, and was betrayed into the one serious failing of his life. Had he escaped this reef, and had his pecuniary position been a little more easy, there is little in Chauncey's lot that I can look back upon and wish it had been other—he being the man he was, and so little capable of conforming himself to alien conditions of life. . . .

Chauncey was so purely intellectual and his intellect so predominantly scientific, with most precise canons of evidence rigidly applied, that it was hardly possible that he should do full justice to natures of a different type, into whose judgments the feelings are always filtering. He was so devoid of all desire to make up his mind on speculative points upon which the evidence left his judgment in doubt, so content to leave such matters unsettled—those of the greatest equally with those of the least moment—that he could not at all understand the state of minds impatient of uncertainty and eager for a decision, at least upon all important questions. Chauncey, in other words, was by intellectual temperament a skeptic, in the best sense of that term, an onlooker who is interested neither to prove nor to disprove, but to judge; and, when there is insufficient material for judging, to hold his mind in suspense—a suspense, however, which contains no element of pain. Upon his chart of the Universe, the *terra incognita* of the not-proven that stretched between the firm ground of the proved and the void of the disproved, included some of the chief beliefs to which mankind has clung; but it should be said also that he admitted the entire rightfulness of the claim of Faith to take possession of any portion of this territory, provided she did it in her own name: there might even be much solid and goodly land there, and not mere mirage of tradition and the emotions; he denied only that it lay within the range of man's experience, and therefore of knowledge in the sense in which he understood and used that term. . . .

In commenting upon Chauncey's character and conduct, I find myself always going back almost at once to that powerful intellectual machinery which was ever weaving his own experience and that of others into theories of Life and the Universe. Yet this does injustice to him and to me. It is not the philosopher, but the friend, that comes so often into my memory—more often, indeed, as time passes than when he first departed from among us. That noble head recalls not so much the massive brain as the sweet smile and the eyes that brightened with enjoyment of every touch of humor. The playfulness of his manner stands out as distinctly as the sedateness and dignity which it lighted up so charmingly. What simple dignity his manners had! Like those of another friend (Dennett), likewise cut off in his prime, with literary gifts as exceptional as Chauncey's in abstract thought, his manners had that stamp of innate nobility which makes, instead of learns, the rules of good breeding. The manners, I need not say, were but the expression of the qualities within. The perfect simplicity of his character, the inconsistency of it with the very idea of an *arrière pensée,* gave a singular attraction to the complexity and profundity of his thinking; but not less admirable was the reserve that never obtruded itself nor gave an opening for obtrusion on the part of others. My wife reminds me how ready he was to condescend in explanations to scientific intellects of low degree; but Chauncey had that genuine superiority, both of mind and character, which is never conscious of differences of degree. It is worth noting, however, what power he possessed, from his perfect mastery of his subjects, for making difficult things plain when he recognized what was a person's need; but an explanation meant to his mind a reference of a particular case to a general law—the more perfect, the higher the generalization—and he paid his pupils the unconscious compliment of supposing that they could keep pace with him, unless they constantly warned him to the contrary.

It was pleasant to see in so masculine an intellect as Chauncey's such thorough appreciation and enjoyment of women, and all that is most characteristic and fine in women. He was certainly catholic in his taste among men; but, as I run over in my mind the women who found a place in his regard, I am struck with the sureness of his instinct for what is charming, refined, and feminine. The friendship of such women was the strongest of testimonies, were testimony needed, to a singular rectitude and purity of soul in Chauncey, and to the native delicacy of spirit and absence of all personal claims which make such relations cordial and easy. Like the friendship of children, which he always inspired, it gives a certain stamp as of sterling quality to the character. The praise of these would have been to Chauncey's ear the final word of commendation, and I will add no other.

II. CHAUNCEY WRIGHT[1]

by William James

If power of analytic intellect pure and simple could suffice, the name of Chauncey Wright would assuredly be as famous as it is now obscure, for he was not merely the great mind of a village—if Cambridge will pardon the expression—but either in London or Berlin he would, with equal ease, have taken the place of master which he held with us. The reason why he is now gone without leaving any work which his friends can consider as a fair expression of his genius, is that his shyness, his want of ambition, and to a certain degree his indolence, were almost as exceptional as his power of thought. Had he, in early life, resolved to concentrate these and make himself a physicist, for example, there is no question but that his would have ranked today among the few first living names. As it was, he preferred general criticism and contemplation, and became something resembling more a philosopher of the antique or Socratic type than a modern *Gelehrter*. His best work has been done in conversation; and in the acts and writings of the many friends he influenced his spirit will, in one way or another, as the years roll on, be more operative than it ever was in direct production. Born at Northampton in 1830, graduating at Harvard in 1852, he left us in the plenitude of his powers. His outward work is limited to various articles in the *North American Review* (one of which Mr. Darwin thought important enough to reprint as a pamphlet in England), a paper or two in the Transactions of the Academy of Arts and Sciences, and a number of critical notices in our own pages—the latest of these being the article entitled "German Darwinism," which we published only two weeks ago. . . . As little of a reader as an educated man well can be, he yet astonished everyone by his omniscience, for no specialist could talk with Chauncey Wright

[1] [From *Nation,* XXI (1875), 194.]

without receiving some sort of instruction in his specialty. This was due to his irrepressible spontaneous habit of subtle thinking. Every new fact he learned set his whole mental organism in motion, and reflection did not cease till the novel thought was firmly woven with the entire system of his knowledge. Of course in this process new conclusions were constantly evolved, and many a man of science who hoped to surprise him with news of a discovery has been himself surprised by finding it already *constructed* by Wright from data separately acquired in this or that conversation with one or other of the many scholars of Cambridge or Boston, most of whom he personally knew so well.

In philosophy, he was a worker on the path opened by Hume, and a treatise on psychology written by him (could he have been spared and induced to undertake the drudgery) would probably have been the last and most accomplished utterance of what he liked to call the British school. He would have brought the work of Mill and Bain for the present to a conclusion. Of the two motives to which philosophic systems owe their being, the craving for consistency or unity in thought and the desire for a solid outward warrant for our emotional ends, his mind was dominated only by the former. Never in a human head was contemplation more separated from desire. Schopenhauer, who defined genius as a cognitive faculty manumitted from the service of the will, would have found in him an even stronger example of his definition than he cared to meet. For to Wright's mode of looking at the universe such ideas as pessimism or optimism were alike simply irrelevant. Whereas most men's interest in a thought is proportioned to its possible relation to human destiny, with him it was almost the reverse. When the mere actuality of phenomena will suffice to describe them he held it pure excess and superstition to speak of a metaphysical whence or whither, of a substance, a meaning, or an end. Just as in cosmogony he preferred Mayer's [2] theory to the nebular hypothesis, and in one of his earliest *North American Review*

[2] [Julius Robert Mayer (1814-1878), German physicist. Cf. Wright's "Physical Theory of the Universe," *Philosophical Discussions*, pp. 1-34.]

articles used the happy phrase "cosmical weather" to describe the irregular dissipation and aggregation of worlds; so, in contemplating the totality of being, he preferred to think of phenomena as the result of a sort of ontologic weather, without inward rationality, an aimless drifting to and fro, from the midst of which relatively stable and so (for us) rational combinations may emerge. The order we observe in things needs *explanation* only on the supposition of a preliminary or potential disorder; and this he pointed out is, as things actually *are* orderly, a gratuitous notion. Anaxagoras,[3] who introduced into philosophy the notion of the νοῦς, also introduced with it that of an antecedent chaos. But if there be no essential chaos, Mr. Wright used to say, an antichaotic νοῦς is superfluous. . . .

Mr. Wright belonged to the precious band of genuine philosophers, and among them few can have been as completely disinterested as he. Add to this eminence his tireless amiability, his beautiful modesty, his affectionate nature and freedom from egotism, his childlike simplicity in wordly affairs, and we have the picture of a character of which his friends feel more than ever now the elevation and the rarity.

[3] [Anaxagoras (*c.* 500 B.C.), Greek philosopher, brought the spirit of philosophical and scientific inquiry from Ionia and firmly established it in Athens before he was banished for contravening the dogmas of the established religion.]